CONSERVATION·ON
trails

A guide to Missouri Department
of Conservation trails

compiled by Teresa Kight, recreation specialist

Serving nature and you

TABLE OF CONTENTS

CONSERVATION trails

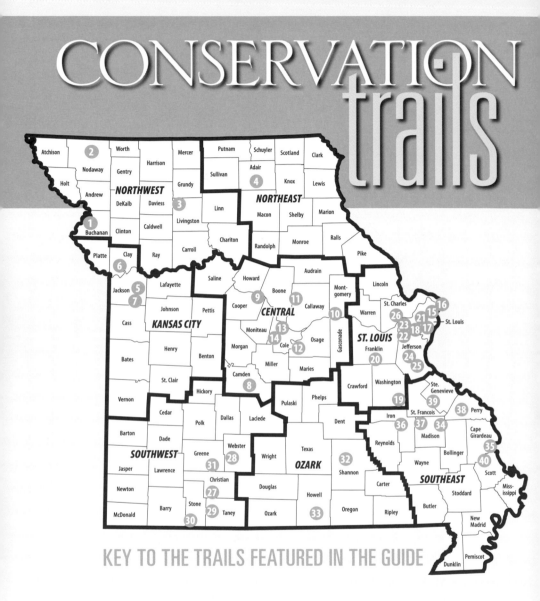

KEY TO THE TRAILS FEATURED IN THE GUIDE

See page 96 for a complete list of conservation area trails.

CONSERVATION DEPARTMENT REGIONAL OFFICES

NORTHWEST
701 James McCarthy Drive
St. Joseph 64507
816-271-3100

NORTHEAST
2500 S. Halliburton
Kirksville 63501
660-785-2420

KANSAS CITY
3424 N.W. Duncan Road
Blue Springs 64015
816-655-6250

CENTRAL
1907 Hillcrest Drive
Columbia 65201
573-884-6861

ST. LOUIS
2360 Hwy. D
St. Charles 63304
636-441-4554

SOUTHWEST
2630 N. Mayfair
Springfield 65803
417-895-6880

OZARK
551 Joe Jones Blvd.
West Plains 65775
417-256-7161

SOUTHEAST
2302 County Park Drive
Cape Girardeau 63701
573-290-5730

PREFACE

The mission of the Missouri Department of Conservation is to protect and manage the fish, forest and wildlife resources of the state, to serve the state's citizens and facilitate their participation in resource management activities, and to provide opportunities for all citizens to use, enjoy and learn about fish, forest and wildlife resources.

The Conservation Department's vision is to have healthy, sustainable plant and animal communities throughout the state for future generations to use and enjoy, and for fish, forest and wildlife resources to be in appreciably better condition tomorrow than they are today.

It is a priority for the Department to develop and maintain its existing lands. Improved disabled access and expanded opportunities for hunters and anglers will help ensure diverse uses of our lands. Managers are enhancing opportunities for compatible activities such as hiking, birding and nature study, so others also may explore and enjoy conservation areas.

This trail guide has been completely revised to highlight 98 trails and trail systems on 40 conservation areas. Many of the trails included in this book are open to foot traffic only. Some are open to horses and bicycles. Trail lengths vary from 0.1 mile to 20 miles, with hiking opportunities that range from easy and level paved paths to difficult and rugged natural-surface trails.

At the end of the book is a list of all designated trails on Conservation Department areas. Maps are available online at www.missouriconservation.org and at regional offices.

For directions to all conservation areas, with and without designated trails, send for a free copy of "Discover Outdoor Missouri" map, by writing to "Discover Outdoor Missouri" map, Missouri Department of Conservation, P.O. Box 180, Jefferson City, MO 65102-0180.

The Department also offers the *Missouri Conservation Atlas*, with county maps and directions to conservation areas. This book can be purchased by going online at www.mdcnatureshop.com or by calling the toll-free number 877-521-8632.

TRAIL TIPS, TOOLS AND RULES

Trails provide access within areas and allow for personal enjoyment, interpretation and a greater understanding of the natural environment. Your visit to a conservation trail will be a pleasant adventure if you invest in some basic planning and preparation:

- Dress comfortably and prepare for possible changes in weather. Appropriate footwear is necessary; sturdy hiking boots are recommended for natural-surface trails.
- Consider using sunscreen and insect repellent in the warmer months.
- Bring along water and a snack for longer hikes.
- A hiking stick can be handy to clear spider webs or debris from across your path, for support on long uphill or downhill stretches, and to provide balance when crossing a stream.
- If you plan to do some exploring, consider carrying a small fanny pack or backpack with topographic maps, compass, camera or binoculars. Field guides will help you identify and learn about plants, birds and animals along the trail.

Follow these general guidelines to help protect the trail and leave it in good condition for the next visitor:

- Respect nature; stay on designated trails. Don't take shortcuts or cut across switchbacks.
- Avoid wet or muddy trails; come back another day when the trails are dry.
- Limit the size of your group to reduce trail impacts.
- Pack out all of your litter.

These tips will help you have a safe and enjoyable experience on the trail:

- Be considerate of other trail users. On shared-use trails you may encounter horseback riders or bicyclists.
- All users should yield to those with disabilities. Hikers and bicyclists should yield to horseback riders, and bicyclists should yield to hikers.
- Help us keep the trails in good condition. Call or write to the area contact to report safety issues or trail maintenance needs.

Read all signs and familiarize yourself with applicable rules and regulations:

- On conservation areas, horses and bicycles are permitted only on trails designated for their use, and on area roads and trails open to vehicular traffic, unless otherwise posted.
- Pets are permitted on many conservation areas, but they must be on a leash or confined at all times. Pets are not permitted at conservation nature centers, Rockwoods Reservation, or on the trail at Painted Rock Conservation Area.
- Hunting and fishing regulations vary from area to area. If you are planning to take part in these activities, obtain a copy of the area brochure or call for specific information on seasons, methods and limits. Also, you can check the Department's website at www.missouriconservation.org for regulation information and maps. Special regulations or restrictions may apply at individual areas.

LANDSCAPE DESCRIPTIONS

Trails on conservation areas allow Missourians access to different types of terrain and biological communities. Use the following descriptions of natural areas, savannas, oak-hickory forests, wetlands and glades to help you understand and appreciate the diverse landscape of Missouri.

Natural Areas

Natural areas are biological communities or geological sites that preserve the natural character, diversity and ecological processes of Missouri's native landscapes. They are permanently protected and managed for the purpose of preserving their natural qualities. Participating agencies agree that Missouri natural areas should encompass the best examples of all our state's natural ecosystems, and that this is the best use for these special lands. Once designated, Missouri natural areas will be protected forever. Their natural values will not be compromised, except for a critical need for which there is no alternative.

Natural area management subscribes to the following three tenets: 1) to invite the public to use, but not damage the area, 2) to restore the natural processes under which the native plants and animals developed, and 3) to eliminate weedy, exotic plant species that compete with the native vegetation. Natural areas are protected from outside threats such as roads, power lines and pollution.

Some of these natural areas are scenic and accessible. Others are remote and must be located on foot with map and compass. Some areas can withstand considerable human traffic without harm. Others easily could be harmed by overuse. Some areas contain native Missouri habitats that were once abundant, such as prairies, streams, oak-hickory forests and limestone glades. Others contain rare or endangered species or natural communities or features that always have been uncommon, such as large springs, natural bridges, fens and sinkhole ponds.

Natural area managers aim to maintain or enhance the natural quality of the ecosystem in a variety of ways. On some areas, natural forces are allowed to shape the plant and animal communities without intervention. However, correcting the results of human influences and disturbances often requires active management. On several natural areas which include prairies, glades, savannas and woodlands, managers use fire, herbicides and selective cutting to restore and maintain natural communities. On other natural areas it is also necessary to eradicate exotic species, manipulate water levels and provide adequate buffer land.

Savannas

Savannas are the transitional zones between open prairies and closed canopy forest. With a mix of forest overstory and grass understory, they contain parts of both. Savannas are distinguished by a tree canopy cover of 10 to 80 percent, the almost complete absence of a shrub layer, and the dominance of prairie grasses and herbs. Because Missouri had abundant presettlement prairies, more than one-third of the state was probably savanna at one time.

Many factors determine which ecosystem will dominate a landscape. Topography, soil and the direction slopes face all have influences on the plants that grow there, but the most important factor is fire, or the lack of it. Research shows fire was common in presettlement Missouri. Prairies often burned once every three years. These prairie fires rolled toward the east into the advance of the eastern forests. The effect was to push the forest back. With the absence of fire, the forest would begin to advance westward. This east/west tug of war continued for thousands of years, and the results were the growth of savannas and the diverse plant groupings they often contain.

The savanna landscape can be highly variable. In prairie transition areas, the trees may be widely scattered or there may be "islands" of closely grouped trees. In forest transition areas, the trees become closely spaced, with the canopy cover reaching 80 percent.

In presettlement time, fires and large herbivores naturally trimmed the lower tree branches to variable heights. The closely spaced trees, interspersed over grasslands devoid of woody understory vegetation, created a "parklike" landscape.

Oak-hickory Forests

More than 30 percent of Missouri is forested, and oaks and hickories outnumber any other tree species in the state. About three-fourths of the trees in our forests are either oak or hickory. The strong, functional woods of these hardwood trees are manufactured into furniture, lumber, flooring and other products. Yet, for many of us, the beauty, recreation, wildlife habitat and water quality these forests provide are more valuable.

Acorns from oaks provide food for wild animals—especially deer, wild turkeys and squirrels. Hickory nuts also are an important food for many species of wildlife. Squirrels, turkeys and ducks all feed on the nuts, which are often preferred to acorns.

There are 21 species of oak and eight species of hickory in Missouri.

Wetlands

Wetlands, our fastest disappearing ecosystem, formerly made up more than one-tenth of Missouri landscape. Many were created by the spring and fall flooding of rivers and streams, which left behind sheets of nutrient-filled water on the rich bottomland soils. Most of Missouri's original wetlands occurred within the floodplains of major rivers. A large percentage of these original natural wetlands have been drained and converted to agriculture or other human development.

Acre for acre, wetlands support more animal and plant life than most any other kind of ecosystem. Ducks, geese and other migratory birds find abundant food when traveling these riverways on their spring and fall migrations. Wetlands are home to plants that are well adapted to life in water. Wetland ecosystems provide a variety of beneficial functions, such as habitat for endangered and threatened species, water quality improvement and storage of stormwater runoff.

Three types of wetlands are marsh, swamp and fen. Marshes are treeless wetlands often lying in low areas in the floodplains of major rivers and streams. They typically contain a mix of open water and emergent vegetation such as cattails, grasses and sedges.

Swamps are something like marshes, but with trees such as silver maples, American elm, black willow, cypress, cottonwoods and river birches. These areas also have shrubs, mosses and herbaceous plants. Sometimes swamps succeed marshes as trees grow in, but they also may develop in the beds of sluggish streams or in floodplains.

Fens and seeps are unusual wetlands that form in Missouri, mostly in the Ozarks at stream terraces and at the base of bluffs. They are fed by ground water, which means their soils stay wet much of the year. Because the water comes from the ground, it may be alkaline or acidic, depending on the local geology.

Glades

In Missouri we use the term glade for naturally occurring, rocky openings, usually surrounded by woodlands. Glades are most common in hilly terrain, where they often occur on south-facing and west-facing slopes. The sun shines more directly on these slopes, creating conditions that are drier and less conducive to woody plant growth than surrounding areas. Some of the plants and animals found in this harsh world are so specialized that they live nowhere else except here. Examples of these are Ashe's juniper, smoke tree, Fremont's leather flower and purple beard-tongue.

Plant and animal life on the glades changes drastically with the seasons. Spring is a time of much activity and color, but summer on the glade brings extreme heat and drought. The plants growing here have special adaptations that help them survive the dry time. Some plants have long, slender tap roots that grow into the cracks of the rock. They have fleshy stems and leaves, and an ability to drop leaves to reduce water loss. Other plants simply grow only during the winter and spring when water is abundant.

Likewise, some of the animals are similar to those of the desert, and cope by restricting their activities when weather conditions are especially harsh. Lizards take refuge in burrows or rock crevices, and scorpions, pygmy rattlesnakes and mice forage at night.

Fire is important to glade ecology and is one of the tools used in glade management. Glade plants and wildlife are adapted to occasional fires, which stimulate the vegetation and keep woody plants such as red cedar in check.

ADOPT-A-TRAIL PROGRAM

The Missouri Department of Conservation's Adopt-A-Trail Program is a volunteer program providing opportunities for hikers, bicyclists and equestrians to assist conservation area staff by monitoring, maintaining and enhancing trails and trailhead facilities.

For more information, visit www.mdc.mo.gov/trails/adopt.htm or write to:
Adopt-A-Trail Coordinator, Wildlife Division, Missouri Department of Conservation, P.O. Box 180, Jefferson City 65102..

BLUFFWOODS CONSERVATION AREA

Nestled in the Missouri River hills of southwestern Buchanan County, this area consists of 2,344 rugged acres blanketed in loess soil—a loose, silty, fertile soil. The Conservation Department acquired the tract in the mid-1970s to protect one of the last large, heavily forested areas in northwest Missouri. Almost 90 percent of the area is hardwood forest, and home to sugar maple, northern red oak, black walnut, pawpaw, Adam-and-Eve orchids, showy orchids and other plants. More than 100 species of woodland wildlife inhabit Bluffwoods. Steep bluffs adjacent to the Missouri River valley provide many vantage points for scenic views. Hikers may see various forestry practices, including tree planting, timber stand improvement and tree harvesting.

Visitors may enjoy all the area has to offer from two major trail systems. The **Forest Nature Trail** is actually a network of three paved trails and one natural-surface trail. From the parking lot off Bethel Road, the 0.2-mile **Prairie Trail** loops around a restored prairie filled with many of the grasses and wildflowers that once grew in the river hills. The 0.3-mile **Meadow Trail** begins at the southeast end of the Prairie Trail. Along the Meadow Trail, watch for wildlife near the forest edge and stream bed. Both of these trails have an asphalt surface and are disabled-accessible.

The **Bluff Trail** is 0.6 miles long, and connects to the south end of the Meadow Trail. Although it is paved, the terrain is too steep for this trail to meet accessibility standards. As you move through the forest, you will encounter an old field, giant oak trees and steep loess hills. At the north end of the trail is a 0.2-mile winding natural-surface connector path called the **Oak Trail**. This leads back to the Prairie Trail and the parking lot.

continued on page 16

BLUFFWOODS CONSERVATION AREA

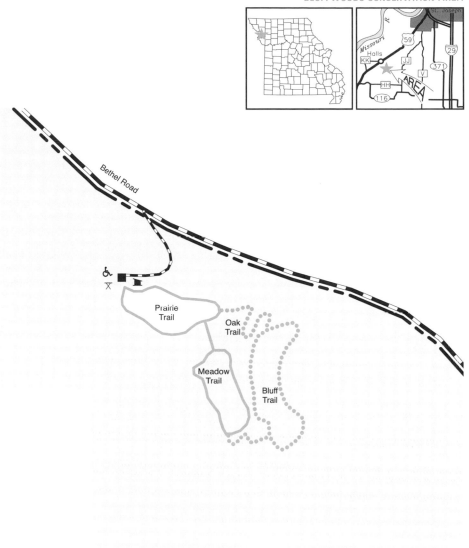

Bethel Road

Prairie Trail

Oak Trail

Meadow Trail

Bluff Trail

N
W — E
S

LEGEND

Boundary
Paved Road
Gravel Road
Hiking Trail
Disabled Accessible Trail
Parking Lot
Picnic Area
Privy
Disabled Accessible
Forest

SCALE

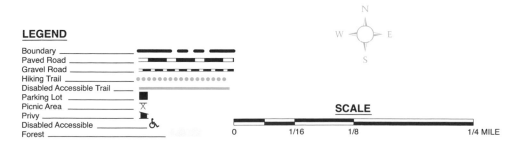

0   1/16   1/8   1/4 MILE

BLUFFWOODS CONSERVATION AREA continued

For a more rugged adventure, sample the trail system on the west side of the area, off 60th Road. From the parking lot, walk in past the picnic area to the beginning of the **Maple Falls Trail**. You'll cover some steep terrain on this 1.5-mile natural-surface trail; you'll also encounter many stream crossings, rock steps and a small wet-weather waterfall.

For a longer hike, cross over to the **Lone Pine Trail**, halfway along the Maple Falls route. This loop trail also covers about 1.5 miles. It provides a very rugged hike, featuring a native grass plot and a scenic overlook high along the bluff top.

From the Lone Pine loop, you can then access the **Turkey Ridge Trail**, a 2-mile loop leading to a second scenic overlook. Be prepared for some steep slopes along this trail. Hikers also may access the Turkey Ridge Trail from the north via a small parking lot on Bluff Road. If you'd like to sample all three trails on your visit, a hike around the outside of each loop will cover 4.5 miles. Depending on your hiking ability and the number of stops you make, this could take two to four hours to complete.

Facilities at the Forest Nature Trail parking lot include a privy and a shelter house with grill and a fire ring. There is a privy and picnic area off the Maple Falls Trail parking lot. Horses and bicycles are not permitted on any of the trails. Primitive camping is allowed at Bluffwoods, and there is a primitive, designated group camping area on the northernmost tract.

Location: From St. Joseph, take Highway 36 west to Highway 59 south. Travel 8.7 miles to the conservation area sign along the highway. Turn left on Bethel Road and drive 1 mile to the Forest Nature Trail parking lot on the right. To reach the more challenging trails, continue south on Highway 59 for 1.2 miles past the area sign. Turn left on Henman Road and drive 0.9 mile to 60th Road. Turn left and travel 0.1 mile to the parking lot on your left.

Contact: Northwest Regional Office, 816-271-3100

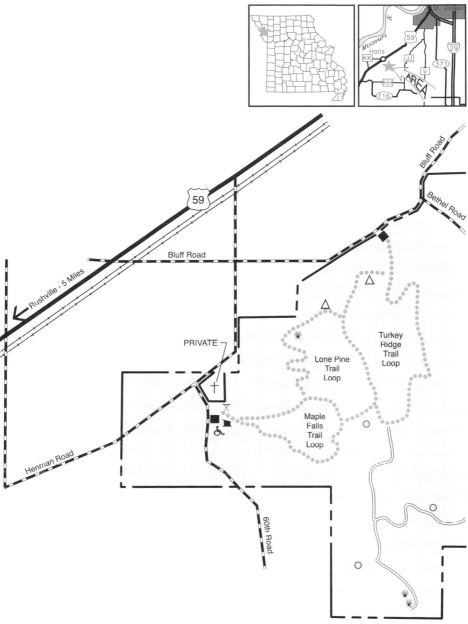

LEGEND

Boundary	
Gravel Road	
Service Road	
Hiking Trail	
Railroad	
Parking Lot	■
Wildlife Water Hole	○
Picnic Area	⅂
Privy	▶
Scenic Overlook	△
Native Grass	☀
Disabled Accessible	♿
Cemetery	†
Forest	

SCALE

0   1/4   1/2   1 MILE

NODAWAY COUNTY COMMUNITY LAKE

This 320-acre area in northwest Missouri features a 73-acre lake, which is stocked with bass, crappie, sunfish and catfish. Most of the land around the lake is pasture and old fields that are being managed for shrubby, early successional habitat. The land east of the lake has been developed into a quail habitat demonstration area. Food plots and warm-season grasses have been established here. Visitors can expect to see birds that frequent brushy habitat such as field sparrows, white-eyed vireos, common yellowthroats and brown thrashers.

A 2.5-mile natural surface **hiking trail** loops around the lake. From the parking lot, head south and follow the wide grass path across the dam. The trail then turns north and weaves through early successional woodland and some fields, with occasional spur trails providing access to the lake. At the north end of the lake, the trail divides. Hikers who veer left will end up at a second parking lot along Highway 148 where primitive camping is allowed. To stay on the main trail, follow the path to the right and continue back to the parking lot. The trail here closely parallels the east side of the lake. Along this portion of the trail are several small fishless ponds and a small remnant prairie. In spring and early summer listen for the western chorus frogs, American toads and Blanchard's cricket frogs that frequent these ponds. The remnant prairie contains the largest population of the rare eared false foxglove in northwestern Missouri. You can see its large pink blooms from mid to late summer.

Allow an hour and a half to walk the loop trail.

Facilities at the lake include a boat ramp, a disabled-accessible fishing jetty and privies.

Location: From Highway 136/48 just north of Maryville, travel 3.7 miles on Highway 148 to the area entrance and lake access parking lot.

Contact: Northwest Regional Office, 816-271-3100

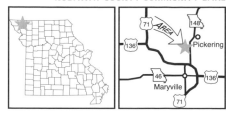

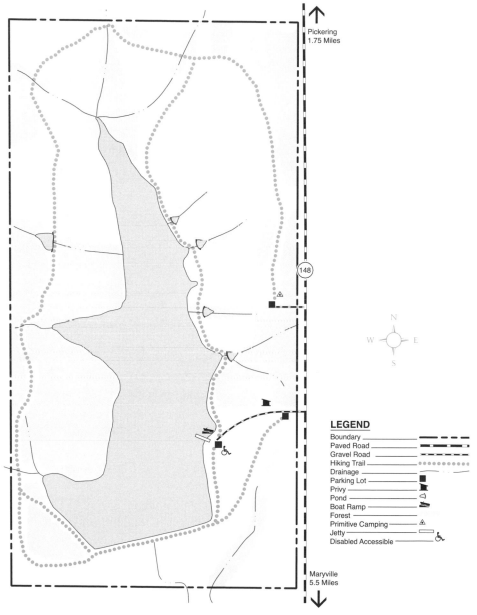

Pickering
1.75 Miles

148

N
W · E
S

Maryville
5.5 Miles

LEGEND

Boundary	
Paved Road	
Gravel Road	
Hiking Trail	
Drainage	
Parking Lot	
Privy	
Pond	
Boat Ramp	
Forest	
Primitive Camping	
Jetty	
Disabled Accessible	

SCALE

0   1/8   1/4 MILE

POOSEY CONSERVATION AREA

The 5,738-acre Poosey Conservation Area, with its combination of hardwood forests and tallgrass prairie, supports thriving plant and animal communities. This portion of the Grand River Valley was one of the last parts of Missouri yielded by the American Indians. In 1833 the remaining Shawnee tribe members left the area, opening it to settlement by people of European extraction, who arrived via Kentucky, Tennessee and Virginia.

Nestled among steep, tree-covered hills in the southern portion of the conservation area is the 192-acre Indian Creek Community Lake. Circling a portion of the lake is the **Green Hills Trail**, open to hiking and bicycling. This linear natural-surface trail winds about 5 miles through oak/hickory woodlands with many scenic lake views. The lake has numerous snags and dead material in the coves, so visitors may see water birds, otters, and aquatic plants and animals.

Trailheads are located on both the east and west sides of the lake. From the east side, enter the woods behind the fishing dock, and then follow the access road across the dam. The trail enters the forest again and weaves up and down rocky hills along an arm of the lake. As the trail crosses a drainage and nears the west side parking lot, take a right to continue low along the arm of the lake, or follow the optional route higher along the hillside. Both paths meet again just before the parking area. Allow two hours round trip to walk the trail between county roads 510 and 515.

For trail users starting from the west side parking lot, head north past the picnic shelter and follow the path along the west side of Indian Creek Lake. Portions of this trail segment are steep with loose, rocky footing. Take your time and enjoy the frequent lake views. After a few miles the trail veers away from the lake and turns west, finishing through grassland and crop fields.

In addition to the Green Hills Trail, more than 20 miles of trails and service roads on the northern half of the area have been designated as a **multi-use trail** system open to hiking, bicycling and horseback riding. Equestrians are permitted on the multi-use trails north of Highway A only. All trails are closed during firearms deer season.

Location: North of Chillicothe, take Highway 190 west for 10 miles to Route U. Travel north 4.5 miles and turn right on County Road 510 to Indian Creek Lake. Follow this road to parking lot No. 14 across from the shelter house and privy. From this parking lot visitors can access the trail to the north and south. The south trail also can be reached from the southeast side lake access. From Route A, at the sign for Indian Creek Lake, follow County Road 515 approximately 1.5 miles to the second gravel road on the right, which leads to the lake access parking lot and trailhead.

Contact: Chillicothe Office, 15368 Liv 2386, Chillicothe 64601, 660-646-6122

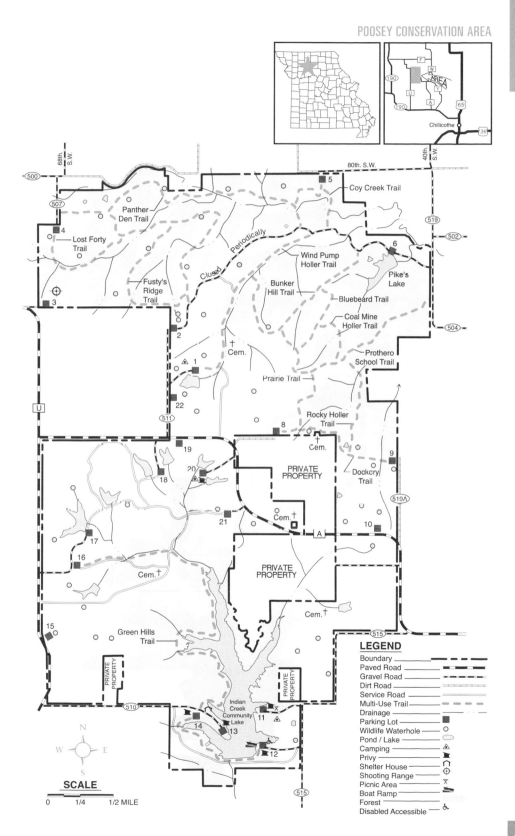

Chillicothe

68th. S.W.
80th. S.W.
40th. S.W.

500
507

5
Coy Creek Trail

Panther
Den Trail

519

4
Lost Forty
Trail

502

6
Pike's
Lake

Wind Pump
Holler Trail

Closed   Periodically

Fusty's
Ridge
Trail

Bunker
Hill Trail

Bluebeard Trail

3

504

2

Coal Mine
Holler Trail

†
Cem.

Prothero
School Trail

1

Prairie Trail

U

22

511

Rocky Holler
Trail

8

†
Cem.

19

9

Dockery
Trail

20

18

519A

21

Cem. †

10

A

PRIVATE
PROPERTY

17

16

Cem. †

PRIVATE
PROPERTY

Cem. †

515

15

Green Hills
Trail

LEGEND

Boundary	
Paved Road	
Gravel Road	
Dirt Road	
Service Road	
Multi-Use Trail	
Drainage	
Parking Lot	■
Wildlife Waterhole	○
Pond / Lake	
Camping	⚠
Privy	
Shelter House	⊕
Shooting Range	
Picnic Area	X
Boat Ramp	
Forest	
Disabled Accessible	♿

PRIVATE
PROPERTY

PRIVATE
PROPERTY

510

Indian
Creek
Community
Lake

X
11

14
13

12

N
W   E
S

SCALE

0   1/4   1/2 MILE

515

SUGAR CREEK CONSERVATION AREA

This 2,609-acre area is primarily forested, with a few open fields on ridges and along Sugar Creek. Around the turn of the century, thousands of forested acres in the region were cleared to meet the demand for mine props and timbers for the coal mining industry in northeast Missouri. Subsequent tree sprouting here was contained by grazing goats before most of the area was allowed to revert back to trees. This accounts for the large continuous stands of similarly aged trees found here. The Conservation Department acquired the original 72 acres of this area as a forest fire lookout tower site, but the tower was never built. Known then as Kirksville Woods, this small area was combined with a 2,536-acre tract purchased in 1974, to create Sugar Creek Conservation Area.

During your visit you may view various forest improvement practices designed to improve wildlife habitat, maintain watershed quality, and enhance tree growth, quality and species composition. Signs of disturbance are only temporary, and the forest will soon return to normal. Wildlife management practices include crop fields to serve as food sources for animals, and harvesting timber to provide improved forage and cover for wildlife. White-tailed deer and wild turkey are abundant on the area, as are numerous songbirds and a variety of mammals. Ruffed grouse, native to Missouri, have been restocked on the area, and a huntable population of the birds can be found here.

The **Ironwood Hollow Foot Trail** is a 2-mile natural-surface loop. The wide and well-marked trail leads through white oak and oak-hickory forests. From the parking lot, the path gradually descends into a valley, where bridges allow for easy creek crossings. Here you will see the small understory tree for which the trail is named. This tree, also known as eastern hop hornbeam, may be identified by its smooth, shreddy-looking bark that closely resembles that of cedar. The trail turns and climbs to follow a forested ridge, then leads back into the valley and up to another ridge top. The final portion of the trail is along a gravel road back to the parking lot.

Horses and bicycles are permitted on a separate, designated **multi-use trail** that forms a 10-mile loop around much of the conservation area. Access to this trail is available from a number of area parking lots.

Primitive camping is allowed on and adjacent to all area parking lots. Walk-in camping is allowed except during the firearms deer and turkey seasons. Walk-in campsites must be at least 100 yards from all public access roads, open fields and parking lots. A disabled-accessible rifle and shotgun range on the west side of the area has 12 shooting benches.

Location: From Kirksville, go south on Highway 63, then west on Highway 11 for 1.5 miles. Turn south on Highway 3 and travel 2.7 miles to Crest Trail. Turn right and drive 0.6 mile; turn right again for 0.3 mile to the parking area on the left.

Contact: Northeast Regional Office, 660-785-2420

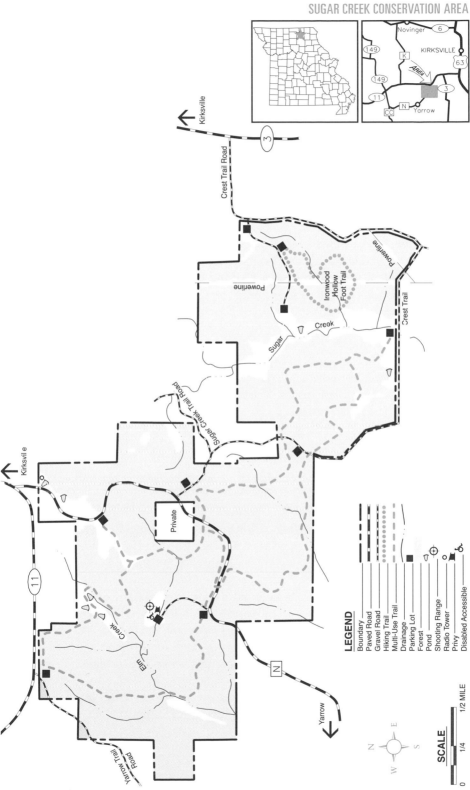

KIRKSVILLE

Novinger 6

149

K

149

11

CC N

Yarrow

63

3

Area

Kirksville

3

Crest Trail Road

Powerline

Powerline

Ironwood Hollow Foot Trail

Sugar Creek

Crest Trail

Sugar Creek Trail Road

Kirksville

Private

11

Elm Creek

N

Yarrow

Yarrow Trail Road

LEGEND

Boundary
Paved Road
Gravel Road
Hiking Trail
Multi-Use Trail
Drainage
Parking Lot
Forest
Pond
Shooting Range
Radio Tower
Privy
Disabled Accessible

N
W   E
S

SCALE

0   1/4   1/2 MILE

✝ BURR OAK WOODS CONSERVATION AREA

This 1,071-acre area, 20 miles east of downtown Kansas City, is composed of a reconstructed prairie, glades, savanna, forest, streams and ponds. More than 70 percent is forested with species such as white oak, northern red oak, black walnut, hackberry, ash, hickory and Kentucky coffeetree. A 33-acre natural area includes an old-growth upland forest. Large Bethany Falls limestone outcrops and scattered boulders add interest to the area. Burr Oak Woods is a wildlife refuge, and the rich diversity of wildlife species includes white-tailed deer, turkey, bobcats, raccoons, coyotes, opossum, fox, hawks and many songbirds. Management of the forest and wildlife is complemented by the conservation education and interpretive programming at the nature center located on site.

There are five nature trails on the area. The 0.7-mile **Missouri Tree Trail** just west of the nature center is a paved, disabled-accessible loop. A short distance in on this trail, you will find a viewing blind that overlooks a prairie. Farther along, the trail travels over a pond and leads to a long viewing platform overlooking a glade.

The 0.5-mile **Discovery Trail** loop is behind the nature center. This trail is paved, but not disabled-accessible due to steep terrain. It features a viewing platform overlooking the interior of a climax oak-hickory forest. A bridge leads up to a prairie, where a connector wood-chip trail leads west to link with the Missouri Tree Trail.

The **Habitat Trail** is a 1.5-mile loop with a wood-chip surface. Points of interest include forest, pond and glade. Interpretive signs introduce visitors to the surrounding habitats and plants and wildlife found there. The trail is wide and mostly level, but has a few steeper sections.

The 1.3-mile **Bethany Falls Trail** passes Burr Oak Creek, goes through the natural area and past a prairie. Interpretive signs highlight the history, forest and wildlife interests along the trail. The most noticeable feature along this trail is the Bethany Falls limestone. One section of trail weaves through these massive chunks of rock outcropping. The trail has a wood-chip surface and has some steep and narrow spots through the rocks.

The 3.3-mile **Hickory Grove Trail** begins at the parking lot for the Habitat Trail and ends at the Bethany Falls Trail parking area. Most of the route is through forest, and midway the trail passes a pond with a viewing blind. The surface is gravel. This is the only area trail on which jogging and running are allowed.

The Conservation Nature Center is a hands-on facility where visitors may learn about nature. Included in the building are live animal exhibits with reptiles and amphibians, a 3,000-gallon aquarium, an indoor wildlife-viewing area, and a 155-seat auditorium. Naturalist-led programs are offered to schools, families and individuals. Prior arrangements are required for programs. Special events are scheduled throughout the year. Two picnic shelters are available. Pets are not permitted on this area.

Location: From I-70 in Blue Springs, travel north on Highway 7 for 1.1 miles, then west on N.W. Park Road to the nature center.

Contact: Burr Oak Woods Conservation Nature Center, 1401 N.W. Park Road, Blue Springs 64015, 816-655-6250

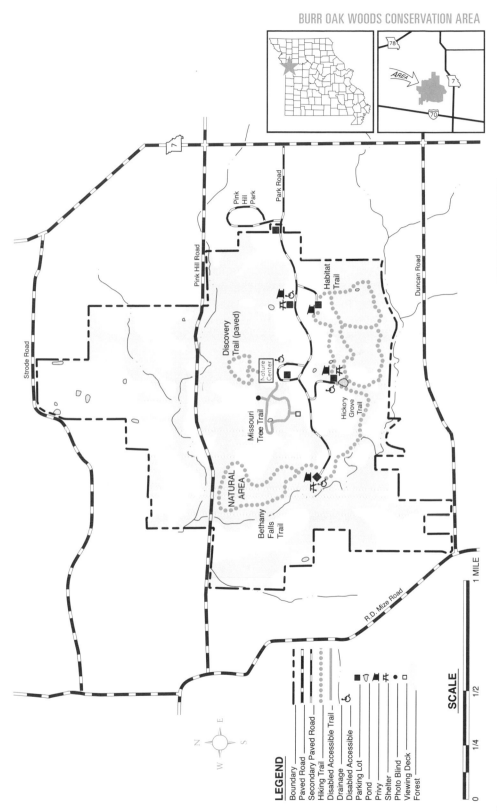

KANSAS CITY

Pink Hill Park

Park Road

Pink Hill Road

Strode Road

Duncan Road

Habitat Trail

Discovery Trail (paved)

Nature Center

Missouri Tree Trail

Hickory Grove Trail

NATURAL AREA

Bethany Falls Trail

R.D. Mize Road

N
W E
S

LEGEND
Boundary
Paved Road
Secondary Paved Road
Hiking Trail
Disabled Accessible Trail
Drainage
Disabled Accessible
Parking Lot
Pond
Privy
Shelter
Photo Blind
Viewing Deck
Forest

SCALE
0   1/4   1/2   1 MILE

25

✳MAPLE WOODS NATURAL AREA

This 39-acre area is owned by the Conservation Department and leased to the City of Gladstone for management and use as a nature preserve. It is a forested oasis in the midst of suburban homes. The rolling terrain is interrupted by rock outcrops and intermittent streams. Natural features include an old-growth upland forest with many spring wildflowers and beautiful fall colors. Sugar maple, red oak, white oak and basswood are the dominant trees.

Woodsia fern, Dutchman's breeches, yellow violet, wild ginger, spring beauty and bloodroot abound in April and early May, when parts of the area are carpeted with May apples. Look for the unusual Indian pipe and two native orchids that emerge from the forest floor. In May and June, the woods provide nesting habitat for scarlet and summer tanagers, parula warblers and a variety of other woodland birds, including woodpeckers. You may hear the call of a barred owl or great-horned owl.

The 1.4-mile natural-surface **Maple Woods Trail** system follows varied terrain across the area. From the parking lot the path rises steeply and follows an old roadbed straight up a rocky hill. You also may veer left just over the bridge by the parking lot for a similarly steep climb to start your hike. Depending on which direction you take, if you stay to the outside of the loop you will cover a bit more than a mile.

A few interior trails bisect the large loop, each roughly from east to west. The northernmost connector runs along the edge of a field. Here you will find a large boulder with a plaque designating the area as a registered natural landmark. The southernmost connector trail follows a contour halfway up a slope, with the field above and stream below. A hike that accommodates all of the area paths will take less than one hour. Watch for rocks and exposed tree roots along this trail, and expect to get your feet muddy at certain times of the year, especially in spring.

There are no facilities at this area. Hiking and nature study are the only activities allowed.

Location: From the intersection of I-435 and I-35 near Claycomo, go north on I-435 to Highway 152. Travel west on Highway 152 to Highway 1 (N. Indiana), then south on Highway 1 a short distance to the stoplight at Maplewoods Parkway/N.E. 80th Street. Turn right on Maplewoods Parkway, then turn left at N. Agnes. Follow N. Agnes 0.7 mile and the road becomes N.E. 76th Street as it rounds the curve. The area parking lot is on the left.

Contact: Kansas City Regional Office, 816-655-6250

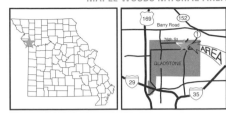

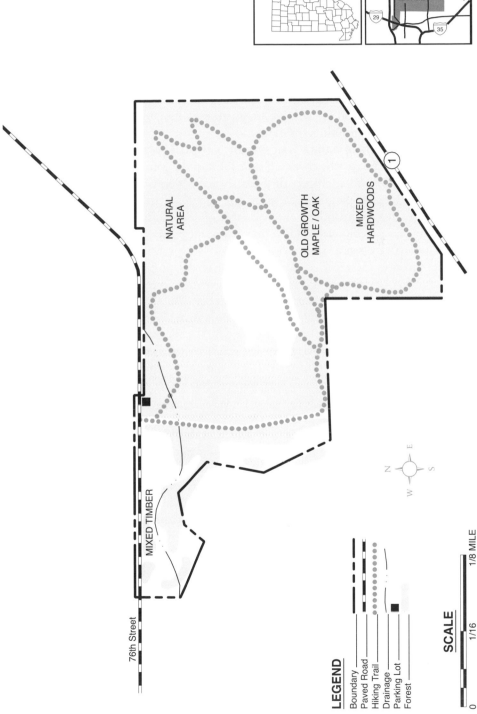

KANSAS CITY

NATURAL AREA

OLD GROWTH MAPLE / OAK

MIXED HARDWOODS

MIXED TIMBER

76th Street

N E S W

LEGEND

Boundary
Paved Road
Hiking Trail
Drainage
Parking Lot
Forest

SCALE

0   1/16   1/8 MILE

JAMES A. REED MEMORIAL WILDLIFE AREA

This 2,603-acre wildlife area is southeast of Kansas City. The Conservation Department began to develop the area and construct its many lakes in 1957. More than 250 acres of water have been impounded to form 12 lakes that range in size from 1 to 42 acres. Most lakes contain largemouth bass, channel catfish, crappie, bluegill, green sunfish, redear sunfish and bullheads. Striped bass hybrids have been stocked in several of the lakes.

Waterfowl, shorebirds and wading birds visit the area, and giant Canada geese nest and spend the winter here. The area also supports good numbers of deer. Crop fields, woodlands, native grass plantings and shrub plantings are managed to provide year-round food for wildlife. A portion of the property has been set aside for a butterfly and hummingbird garden.

The **Shawnee Trace Nature Trail** system is located on the east side of the area. These natural-surface paths cover 2.5 miles. From the informational bulletin board at the trailhead, a wood-chip path leads into the woods and crosses a branch of Big Creek. The trail parallels the creek for about 0.6 mile, crossing it five more times. Along this stretch hikers have a couple of opportunities to shorten their hike by turning left on connector trails. Stop to admire the mature black walnut and chinquapin oak trees near the creek.

After crossing the creek at the south end of the property, you may veer right on a loop that passes through old fields, alternately, you may choose to turn left where the path splits. In this direction you'll see a small glade, and if you follow the trail up a limestone bluff you'll enjoy expansive views of the forest and creek below. Whichever trail sections you choose, you'll walk through a variety of habitats and get a good workout across the varied terrain. There are a few steep, rough and narrow sections along this trail system, so be prepared for a moderate hike. A trip around the outside loop may take about one hour.

Rest-room facilities and a picnic area are near the office, and privies can be found at a number of lake parking lots on the area. Visitors may walk the interior roads and 15-mile **multi-use trail** system, in addition to the hiking trail system. Horses and bicycles are allowed on the multi-use trail system during daylight hours only. The area is open from 6 a.m. to 10 p.m. from April 1 to Sept. 30, and from 6 a.m. to 7 p.m. from Oct. 1 to March 31. The office has wildlife mounts and two small tanks that display fish found in the area's lakes. Office hours are 8 a.m. to 5 p.m. daily except for Thanksgiving, Christmas and New Year's Day. Check at area office for hunting seasons and times.

Location: From Lee's Summit, take Highway 50 east to RA (Ranson Road). Go south 1.5 miles to the area entrance on the left. To reach the Shawnee Trace Nature Trails, travel east on the area road for 1.5 miles to the Bodarc Lake parking area on your right.

Contact: James A. Reed Memorial Wildlife Area, 13101 S.E. Ranson Road, Lee's Summit 64082, 816-622-0900

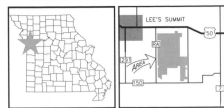

KANSAS CITY

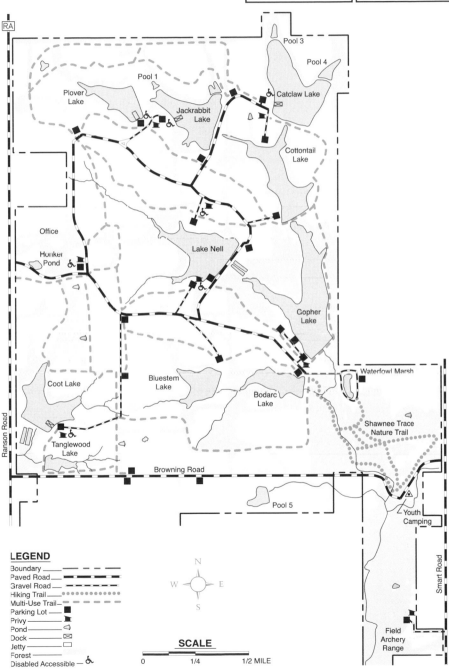

LEGEND

Boundary
Paved Road
Gravel Road
Hiking Trail
Multi-Use Trail
Parking Lot — ■
Privy — ⌐▪
Pond — ◁
Dock — ⊠
Jetty — ▭
Forest
Disabled Accessible — &

N
W — E
S

SCALE

0   1/4   1/2 MILE

Also known as the Conservation Department's Lake of the Ozarks office, the Camdenton office serves Camden, Miller and Morgan Counties. The office site and surrounding acreage was purchased in 1941 as a fire tower location. The original tower was replaced with the present steel tower in 1983.

This area is in a transition zone between the prairies to the northwest and the Ozark forest to the southeast. Plant and animal communities here have features from both forest and prairie, resulting in a mix of trees and prairie plants known as savanna. The geology of the area is characterized by thick limestone rock, both near the surface and many feet below. Rainfall dissolves the rock and forms underground streams. Caves are common throughout this region.

Located high above the Niangua arm of the Lake of the Ozarks, the 1.2-mile **Forest and Savanna Trail** consists of two segments. The beginning segment is paved and disabled-accessible. This linear trail begins at the picnic area and features interpretive signs and scenic overlooks.

The remaining segment loops through the forest and is surfaced with wood chips. Along this portion of trail, hikers are exposed to a mosaic of habitats and features found in the Ozark woodlands. The forest is dominated by oak tree species, and some mixed hickory species. Oak-hickory forests require direct sunlight to thrive. Benches are located along the trail.

Allow one-half hour to walk the loop trail, which dips into deep valleys and winds up steep hills. Bicycles and horses are not permitted on the trail. Visitors may also use the picnic area and climb a portion of the fire tower in front of the conservation office.

Location: The office is 2.25 miles north of the junction of highways 54 and 5 in Camdenton. From Highway 5, turn left on Thunder Mountain Road (Lake Road 5-88). The office is about 0.75 mile on the right.

Contact: Camdenton Conservation Service Center, 783 Thunder Mountain Road, Camdenton 65020, 573-346-2210

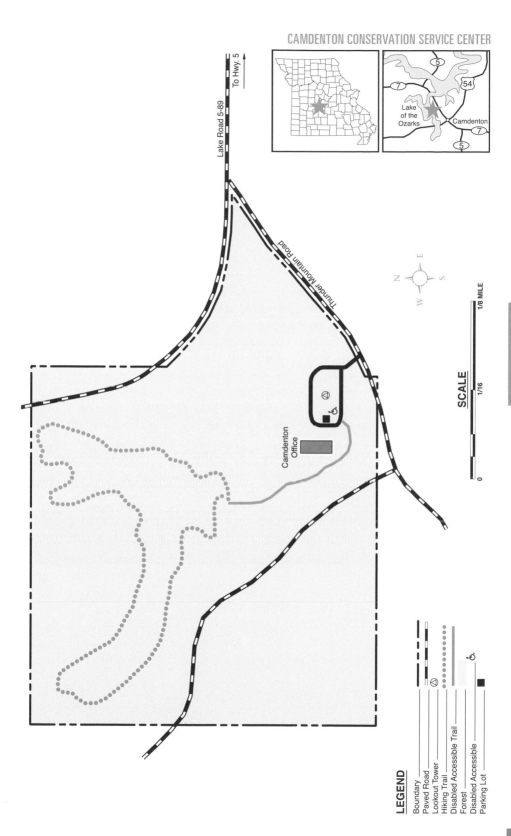

CAMDENTON CONSERVATION SERVICE CENTER

Lake Road 5-89
To Hwy. 5

Thunder Mountain Road

Lake of the Ozarks
Camdenton

5
54
7
7
5

N
E
W
S

SCALE

0   1/16   1/8 MILE

CENTRAL

Camdenton Office

LEGEND

Boundary
Paved Road
Lookout Tower
Hiking Trail
Disabled Accessible Trail
Forest
Disabled Accessible
Parking Lot

✳ DIANA BEND CONSERVATION AREA

In the past, this 1,343-acre area was intensively farmed. About 30 percent of the area is now regenerating cottonwoods and willows. A 3-acre blew hole on the west portion of the area provides walk-in fishing. Diana Bend Conservation Area has the Missouri River as its south boundary, Moniteau Creek and the town of Rocheport to the east, and the Katy Trail State Park to the north. The area is flooded opportunistically, depending on precipitation and Missouri River levels.

Two trails allow visitors to explore a portion of the conservation area. Both trails are open to foot traffic only. The **Boardwalk Trail** is a 0.1 mile disabled-accessible trail. From the Katy Trail just before the MKT tunnel, bear left and follow a short gravel path south to the wood boardwalk. The boardwalk parallels a steep rock face as it approaches a levee and a large viewing platform. The boardwalk then continues along the front of the bluff and zig-zags down to a wildlife viewing/hunting blind. Watch for migratory shorebirds, herons and other waterfowl in the wetland.

Steps lead from the viewing platform to the **Bluff Trail**, a steep natural and wood chip surfaced trail. The trail climbs to the top of the bluff, ending at a viewing platform high above the wetlands. Below and to the north, underneath the hillside, is the MKT tunnel. This 243-foot long stone-arched tunnel was the only tunnel on the entire Missouri, Kansas & Texas Railroad. The railroad came to Rocheport in 1893, and trains ran until 1986. The view from the platform extends out to portions of nearby Overton Bottoms Conservation Area, the Big Muddy National Wildlife Refuge and the Missouri River. The Lewis and Clark expedition camped near here in 1804. Benches midway up the hill and at the top provide convenient resting places.

A segment of the **Katy Trail State Park** is adjacent to the conservation area. This 225-mile long rail-trail, including the tunnel, is managed by the Department of Natural Resources and is open to both hiking and bicycling.

Location: From I-70 at Rocheport (Exit 115), head north and follow Highway 240 for 2 miles. Turn left on Pike Street to the Katy Trail State Park parking lot. Walk west on the Katy Trail about 0.5 mile and turn left just past the bridge over Moniteau Creek.

Contact: Central Regional Office, 573-884-6861

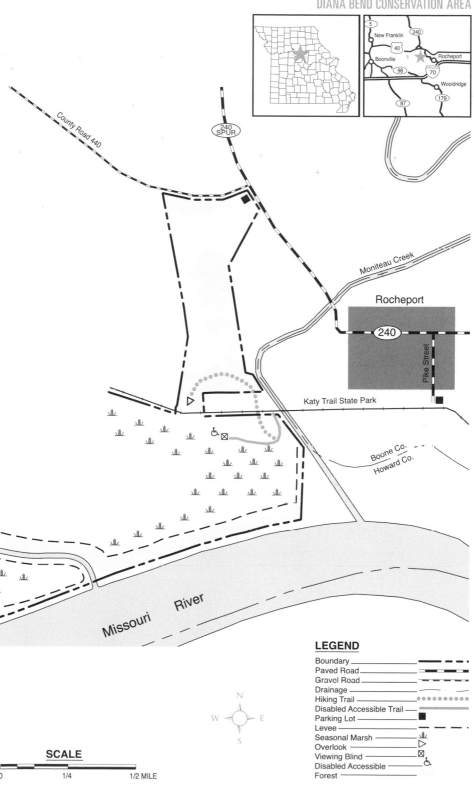

CENTRAL

Missouri State map with star marker

New Franklin 5
240
40
Rocheport
Boonville
98
70
Wooldridge
87
179

County Road 440

240 SPUR

Moniteau Creek

Rocheport
240
Pike Street

Katy Trail State Park

Boone Co.
Howard Co.

Missouri River

LEGEND

Boundary	
Paved Road	
Gravel Road	
Drainage	
Hiking Trail	
Disabled Accessible Trail	
Parking Lot	■
Levee	
Seasonal Marsh	
Overlook	▷
Viewing Blind	⊠
Disabled Accessible	
Forest	

SCALE

0   1/4   1/2 MILE

N
W — E
S

GRAND BLUFFS CONSERVATION AREA

Grand Bluffs Conservation Area is in southern Montgomery County, near the town of Bluffton. This 223-acre area features a stretch of dolomite bluffs overlooking the Missouri River. They are a portion of a spectacular and scenic 2-mile stretch of bluffs, originally formed by the river, which is now 0.25 mile to the south. Synthiana Creek flows through the lower portion of the area.

From a parking lot just off a county road, the 1-mile natural surface **Grand Bluffs Trail** takes you to the top of a 300-foot dolomite bluff. As the trail ascends, you'll pass through a sugar maple/oak forest. The trail then crosses over a level ridge top where a farmstead once set. The land is now managed to revert to an oak savanna natural community. The trail then heads down a slight hill passing through an oak woodland with scattered glades and ends at the edge of a tall bluff where some prairie remnant plants remain. Bluffs in this area were noted in the journals of Lewis and Clark. At trail's end is an overlook deck where visitors can rest and observe spectacular views of the bottomland fields and Missouri River below.

Bird viewing is a popular activity on the area. Turkey vultures fly over the bluffs in the spring, putting the viewer within feet of this large avian. You can watch waterfowl and eagles during migration. Other birds seen on the area include wild turkey, ruffed grouse, scarlet tanager, woodthrush, indigo bunting, yellow breasted chat, eastern kingbird and Baltimore oriole.

This trail is open to hiking only and has some very steep sections. The first half of the trail is an easement—land on both sides of the trail is private property. Please remain on the trail until within the boundary of Grand Bluffs Conservation Area.

Location: From the junction of highways 63 and 54 north of Jefferson City, take Highway 94 east for 34.1 miles. Turn left on County Road 291 and travel north 0.3 mile to a parking lot and trailhead on the right.

Contact: Central Regional Office, 573-884-6861

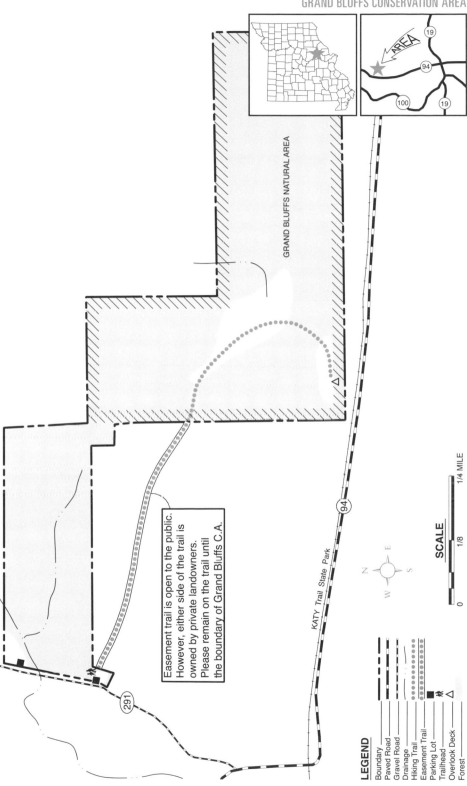

GRAND BLUFFS NATURAL AREA

AREA

KATY Trail State Park

94

291

Easement trail is open to the public.
However, either side of the trail is
owned by private landowners.
Please remain on the trail until
the boundary of Grand Bluffs C.A.

N
W — E
S

SCALE

0   1/8   1/4 MILE

LEGEND
Boundary
Paved Road
Gravel Road
Drainage
Hiking Trail
Easement Trail
Parking Lot
Trailhead
Overlook Deck
Forest

CENTRAL

LITTLE DIXIE LAKE CONSERVATION AREA

This 733-acre area was acquired in 1957 when Owl Creek was dammed to create Little Dixie Lake. The 205-acre lake is managed primarily for sport fishing, with largemouth bass, bluegill, redear sunfish, white crappie and channel catfish as the principle game fish. Prior to Conservation Department ownership, much of the property had been grazed. Today, the area's oak-hickory forests have heavy undergrowth, and pastures that were once open have reverted to various stages of old-field habitat. Stands of warm-season grasses and other prairie plants are managed by prescribed burns. Food plots are planted for deer, turkey and other animals. Numerous small, fishless ponds have been constructed for woodland wildlife. On the lake you may see wintering geese, often in flocks of 500 to 1,000 birds. Unusual visitors to the area include white-winged scoters, ospreys, bald eagles, double-crested cormorants and common loons.

Three trails can be found on the area. The **Dixie Woods Nature Trail** is a paved, disabled-accessible loop trail about 0.4 mile long. Interpretive signs relate the history of the area and describe several natural communities.

The 4.5-mile **Shoreline Trail** stretches from a parking lot on the area's northwest edge, south across the dam to the disabled-accessible facilities, then continues along the lake's east side. This natural-surface trail is well-marked and weaves through forest and field, with many close views of the lake. A 2-mile hike from the area's main parking lot heading north to the west parking lot will take about one hour.

The **Boundary Trail** follows a 6-mile field road that encircles most of the conservation area. This trail is wide and mostly level, and provides occasional lake views. It passes through several habitats including forest, woodland, old field and prairie restorations. Allow at least three hours to walk the entire loop, which also is open to bicycles.

Camping is not permitted on this area, but visitors can enjoy the picnic areas available at three lake-access parking lots. Anglers may take advantage of a disabled-accessible fishing jetty and floating dock.

Location: From Columbia, take I-70 east 8 miles to exit 137. Follow Route J south 3.5 miles, turn left on RA to the main parking lot. From here you can access the Shoreline and Boundary trails. To reach the Dixie Woods Nature Trail from RA, follow County Road 228 east, turn left on County Road 246, then left on County Road 248.

Contact: Central Regional Office, 573-884-6861

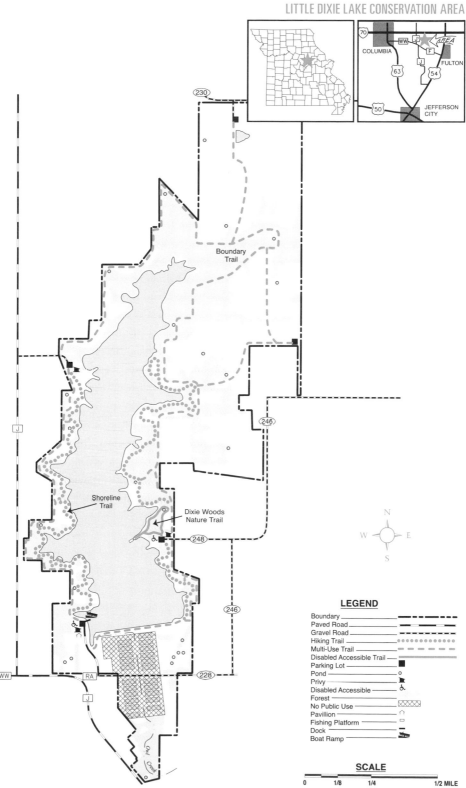

LITTLE DIXIE LAKE CONSERVATION AREA

COLUMBIA

FULTON

JEFFERSON
CITY

230

Boundary
Trail

246

Shoreline
Trail

Dixie Woods
Nature Trail

248

246

228

Owl Creek

CENTRAL

N
W · E
S

LEGEND

Boundary ——————
Paved Road ——————
Gravel Road ——————
Hiking Trail ——————
Multi-Use Trail ——————
Disabled Accessible Trail ——————
Parking Lot —————— ■
Pond —————— ○
Privy ——————
Disabled Accessible —————— &
Forest ——————
No Public Use ——————
Pavillion —————— ⌂
Fishing Platform —————— □
Dock ——————
Boat Ramp ——————

SCALE

0   1/8   1/4   1/2 MILE

✳ PAINTED ROCK CONSERVATION AREA

This property was purchased in 1877 by a group of Jefferson City dignitaries, who named it the Painted Rock Country Club. Their successors sold the property in 1946, and the Conservation Department purchased the land from a private individual in 1981. The 1,490-acre area shows evidence of occupation by Native Americans as early as 9,000 years ago. An Indian burial cairn, along the interpretive trail, was constructed between 500 and 1,500 years ago.

The Osage River—the largest Ozark river in Missouri—borders the property on the west. It supports a mixture of Ozark and big river fauna, including the federally endangered pink mucket mussel and the state-endangered elephant ear mussel. Six ponds in the oak-hickory-sugar maple forest are managed primarily for wildlife. Timber harvesting is managed to improve wildlife habitat, and 60 acres of open land serve as wildlife food plots on a crop rotation basis.

The 1.6-mile **Osage Bluff Scenic Trail** winds through the forest and along high river bluffs. Observation decks on the bluffs allow for expansive views of the Osage River. A few benches along the route provide additional resting spots. From the trailhead, the path leads through the forest and down to the first observation deck, which overlooks Bloody Island to the north. The trail weaves along the contours of the land down into hollows and across a stream.

Where the trail drops down to the river bottom, watch for woodland songbirds and enjoy trillium, bloodroot and other wildflowers in spring. The south overlook, high upon a 140-foot cliff, provides a sweeping view of the river valley. Turkey vultures soar along the bluffs in spring and summer, and you may see bald eagles flying over the Osage River in winter. A great blue heron rookery is within the forest.

Along the trail route you will pass an impressive outcropping composed of three different rock types—dolomite, dolomite/purplish chert and sandstone. Most of the trail tread is 1 to 2 feet wide, with a rocky surface and steep in spots. Use caution and stay on the designated path at all times. An interpretive brochure is available at the trailhead. Allow one and a half hours for a leisurely walk, with time to stop and enjoy the views.

Pets are not allowed on the Osage Bluff Scenic Trail. A gravel road 1.2 miles south of the first parking lot leads to the Painted Rock Lake parking area and a privy. Primitive camping is allowed at a number of designated sites on the area.

Location: From Jefferson City, travel east on Highway 50, south on Highway 63 for 3 miles, go south on Highway 133 for 6.4 miles to the entrance road on the right. Follow the gravel road 0.5 mile to the parking lot and trailhead.

Contact: Central Regional Office, 573-884-6861

Jefferson City

54
50
133
63
52

AREA

CENTRAL

Osage
Bluff
Scenic
Trail

RIVER

OSAGE

133

N
W E
S

LEGEND

Boundary
Paved Road
Gravel Road
Service Road
Hiking Trail
Drainage
Parking Lot
Privy
Primitive Camping
Pond
Lake
Forest

SCALE

0   1/8   1/4   1/2MILE

☀RUNGE CONSERVATION NATURE CENTER

Interpretive exhibits and hiking opportunities abound at this 112-acre area just west of downtown Jefferson City. Experience Missouri's varied habitats through walks on the nature center trails, or go inside to see the displays. You will learn about rivers, streams, forests, glades and other Missouri habitats. You also can view wildlife from an expansive window that overlooks a feeding station. Expect to see a variety of songbirds, white-tailed deer, eastern chipmunks and squirrels. Indoor facilities include a 3,400-gallon aquarium with native Missouri fish, a 200-seat auditorium, three classrooms, nature library, gift shop and a spacious lobby within the exhibit gallery.

On the grounds surrounding the building, five trails pass through a variety of habitat types. You may walk through upland forest, a savanna, glade and prairie. You'll also see several ponds, a marsh and an interminttent stream. Watch for turtles, frogs and dragonflies in the small marsh, and for bluebirds and deer near the savanna. In the summer you'll see the tallgrass prairie planting come to life with forbes like blazing star and pale purple coneflower. Tree identification tags describe many native tree species along trail routes. Watch for deer or red fox crossing the trails through the woods.

The entrance to the **Naturescape Trail** is near the bus parking lot. This 0.3-mile trail is accessible to people with disabilities. Interpretive signs along the trail route describe how to turn your backyard into a wildlife sanctuary. Large, handsome oaks provide food, shade and homes for the abundant wildlife found along this trail. The trail ends at a landscaped area behind the nature center, where you may see various plantings and methods for attracting backyard wildlife.

Just to the south of the Naturescape Trail entrance is the trailhead for the 0.9 mile **Raccoon Run Trail**. This is the longest and most diverse trail. After passing beneath the fire tower, you will hike alongside a savanna under restoration and a tall grass prairie. Look for indigo buntings and variety butterflies and prairie wildflowers. A short spur trail leads to a viewing platform that overlooks a pond—home to many reptiles, amphibians and herons, and a watering hole for deer and raccoons. The 0.3-mile **Bluestem Ridge Trail** weaves through the central portion of the Raccoon Run loop, bisecting the prairie and mixed hardwood forest.

The 0.5-mile **Towering Oak Trail** begins on the northeast end of the parking lot. This natural-surface trail is very steep in spots, and takes its name from the huge oak trees in the forest along the route. The 0.3-mile linear **Moss Rock Trace Trail** forms a link between the Towering Oak and Raccoon Run trails. It winds through a scenic stream and passes by a north-facing glade. All trails connect to form multiple loops and provide a number of different hiking options.

Programs and activities are scheduled throughout the year; reservations may be required. In addition to nature center facilities, there is an outdoor pavilion with restrooms and drinking water. Pets, bicycles, jogging and skating are not permitted.

Location: In Jefferson City, take Highway 50 west to Highway 179 north and travel 0.3 mile to the nature center entrance on the left.

Contact: Runge Conservation Nature Center, P.O. Box 180, Jefferson City 65102-0180, 573-526-5544

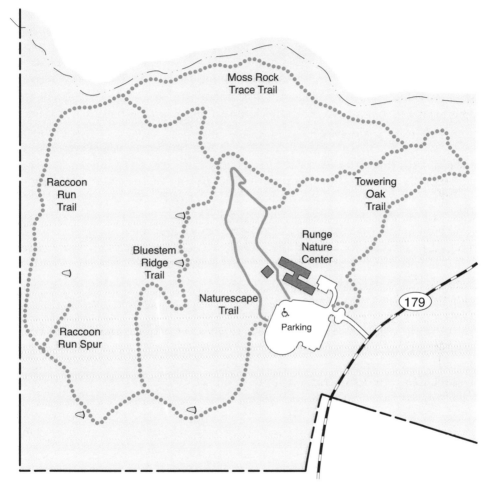

CENTRAL

Moss Rock
Trace Trail

Raccoon
Run
Trail

Towering
Oak
Trail

Bluestem
Ridge
Trail

Runge
Nature
Center

Naturescape
Trail

179

Parking

Raccoon
Run Spur

LEGEND

Boundary	———
Paved Road	———
Drainage	～～
Hiking Trail	••••••
Disabled Accessible Trail	———
Forest	
Disabled Accessible	♿
Pond	◁

N
W ✦ E
S

SCALE

0   100'   200'   400'   800 Feet

41

SCRIVNER ROAD CONSERVATION AREA

Winegar Lake is a central feature of this 919-acre area, which also includes more than 2 miles of frontage along South Moreau Creek. Much of the area consists of rolling upland hills. The dominant vegetation is mostly grassland and brush, but the area includes stands of oak-hickory forest intermixed with cedar thickets. This land was once a cattle farm and extensively grazed. It is now managed for wildlife and public recreation. Management practices include prescribed burning, natural area restoration, and the planting of crops and food plots for wildlife.

The 8.5-mile **Moreau Creek Trail** system consists of a number of interconnected loops. With the exception of portions through forest, most of the wide trail is mowed grass. From the parking lot on the southwest portion of the area, head north and the trail splits a couple of times. If you stay to the left you'll have a nice view of Winegar Lake. Following this path to the north portion of the conservation area, hikers can veer right at the next trail junction and head south again for a 3-mile loop back to the parking area.

For longer hikes, explore the central and eastern trail segments. By staying to the outside of the loops you may circle the area, encountering more stream crossings, ponds, South Moreau Creek and areas of scattered timber. The designated trails also are open to horses from May 15 through Sept. 30 each year. Bicycles are allowed only on roads open to vehicles.

On the south central portion of the area, there is a target shooting range for shotgun, pistol and rifle. There is a privy at the shooting range parking lot. Camping is permitted within 50 feet of two designated parking areas.

Location: From Jefferson City, travel west on Route C to Russellville, then south on Route AA for 2 miles. Turn left on Scrivner Road and drive 1.5 miles to Scott Lane. Turn left and travel 1 mile to the parking area on the left. The trail can be reached from three other area parking lots.

Contact: Central Regional Office, 573-884-6861

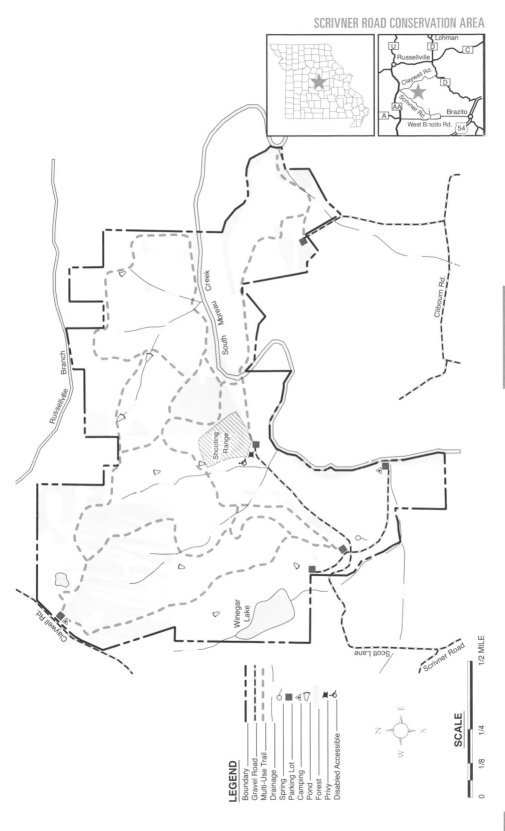

CENTRAL

LEGEND
Boundary
Gravel Road
Multi-Use Trail
Drainage
Spring
Parking Lot
Camping
Pond
Forest
Privy
Disabled Accessible

SCALE
0   1/8   1/4   1/2 MILE

BELLEFONTAINE CONSERVATION AREA

The Bellefontaine Conservation Area provides an opportunity for urban fishing, educational and interpretive facilities close to St. Louis. This site has two walking trails. A 0.3-mile **disabled-accessible asphalt trail** leads from the north parking lot to Bluegill Lake, which is stocked with largemouth bass, bluegill and redear sunfish. A **second trail** is surfaced with wood chips and loops approximately 1.75 miles around the perimeter of the area.

Public fishing is allowed at Bluegill Lake, but the Hybrid and Catfish ponds are reserved for aquatic resource education programs. A disabled-accessible sidewalk leads to these ponds. Facilities on site include a covered pavilion and a rest-room building with drinking fountain. Bicycles are not permitted on the trails, and pets are not allowed on this area.

Location: From I-270 east, take the Highway 367 exit (Exit 31A) in Bellefontaine Neighbors. Travel south to the first traffic signal (entrance to Missouri Veterans Home) and turn left. Turn left again into the conservation area.

Contact: Columbia Bottom Conservation Area, 801 Strodtman Road, St. Louis 63138, 314-877-6019

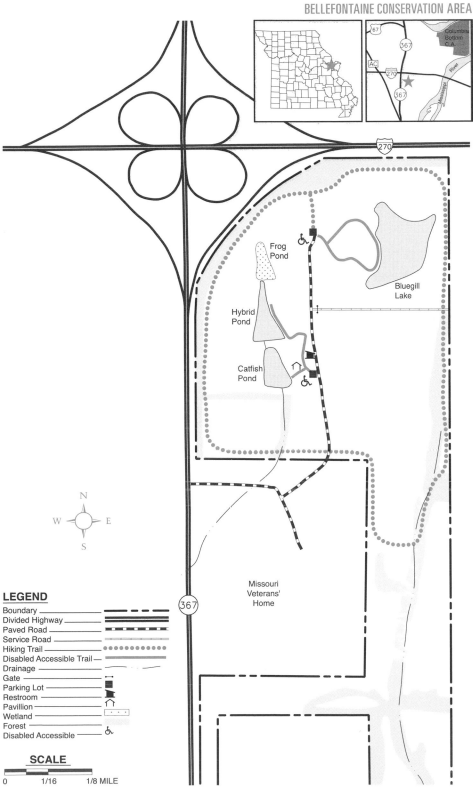

Frog Pond

Bluegill Lake

Hybrid Pond

Catfish Pond

Missouri Veterans' Home

ST. LOUIS

N
W — E
S

LEGEND

Boundary	
Divided Highway	
Paved Road	
Service Road	
Hiking Trail	
Disabled Accessible Trail	
Drainage	
Gate	
Parking Lot	
Restroom	
Pavillion	
Wetland	
Forest	
Disabled Accessible	𝖼

SCALE

0   1/16   1/8 MILE

Columbia Bottom Conservation Area is in north St. Louis County at the confluence of the Missouri and Mississippi rivers. The Conservation Department purchased this 4,318-acre area in 1997 to create an urban conservation area. Columbia Bottom is managed for a mosaic of habitats including shallow wetlands, bottomland hardwoods, prairie and cropland. These habitats attract a variety of resident and migratory wildlife.

Before heading out to the trails on this area, stop at the visitor center to view river and wetland displays. Area maps and other publications are available inside. In front of the visitor center is the first of nine exploration stations on the area. The stations provide information on a feature or habitat found at Columbia Bottom. Colorful tile mosaic artwork accompanies the interpretive information at each station. A 4.5-mile paved road winds east through the area, with small parking lots at each station. The main road ends at a parking area where another short walk leads to an observation platform at the confluence of the Missouri and Mississippi rivers.

The 4.75-mile **Confluence Trail** is a crushed limestone trail open to hiking and bicycling. Access to this trail is available from a parking lot just below the visitor center, the lot at the boat ramp, from parking lots along the roadway between these two locations, and from the confluence parking area. The Confluence Trail follows a levee along the Missouri River and then curves further into the area with the forest on one side and fields and wetlands on the other.

The **River's Edge Trail** is a 3-mile natural surface hiking trail through the bottomland forest along the Missouri river. It begins just east of the boat ramp and ends at the confluence observation platform. Numerous scenic river views can be found along the trail. Bicycles are not permitted on this trail.

A boat ramp is provided on the Missouri River, and there is plenty of fishing opportunity on the banks of the Missouri and Mississippi rivers. Restrooms and a drinking fountain are available in the visitor center, which is open Wednesday through Sunday. Privies are available at the boat ramp and confluence parking lots.

Location: From I-70 in St. Louis, take I-270 north/east to the last Missouri exit at Riverview Drive (Exit 34). Drive north for 2.8 miles to the area entrance on the right (Riverview Drive changes to Columbia Bottom Road, then Strodtman Road).

Contact: Columbia Bottom Conservation Area, 801 Strodtman Road, St. Louis 63138, 314-877-6019

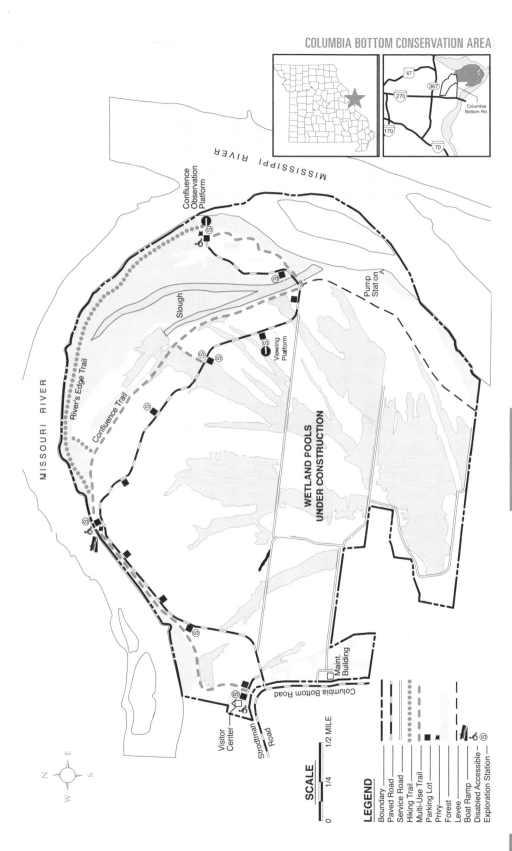

COLUMBIA BOTTOM CONSERVATION AREA

MISSISSIPPI RIVER

MISSOURI RIVER

Confluence Observation Platform

Slough

River's Edge Trail

Confluence Trail

Pump Station

Viewing Platform

WETLAND POOLS UNDER CONSTRUCTION

Maint. Building

Columbia Bottom Road

Visitor Center

Strodtman Road

Columbia Bottom Rd.

ST. LOUIS

SCALE

0   1/4   1/2 MILE

LEGEND

Boundary
Paved Road
Service Road
Hiking Trail
Multi-Use Trail
Parking Lot
Privy
Forest
Levee
Boat Ramp
Disabled Accessible
Exploration Station — Ⓢ

This area was originally part of a large estate owned by members of the Lemp family. The family owned a large St. Louis brewery around the turn of the 20th century. Over the last 100 years the area was used as an exotic animal breeding area for the St. Louis Zoo, a riverside resort, and a public swimming pool and tennis club. The property is now leased by the Conservation Department and is currently operated in partnership with the City of Kirkwood.

The topography of the area allows for a diverse mix of upland hardwoods along the ridges and bottomland species in the valley and along the Meramec River, which is along the western boundary of the area. Upland hardwood forest tree species include white oak, red oak, post oak, shagbark hickory and sugar maple. Understory trees include roughleaf dogwood, redbud and pawpaw. Species in the bottomland areas include elm, boxelder, silver maple, American sycamore and white oak.

The area offers a rich diversity of wildlife species. Deer, squirrels, raccoons, coyotes, opossum and fox can be seen, as well as songbirds and various species of hawks. During the winter months you may catch a glimpse of an American bald eagle soaring above the Meramec River.

Two trails allow visitors to explore the area. A 0.5 **paved trail** has several loops and is disabled-accessible. The 1-mile **Bluff Creek Trail** offers a more robust hiking opportunity, with some steep slopes and long vistas of the Meramec River Valley.

Location: From the junction of I-44 and I-270 in St. Louis County, take I-44 east to the Watson Road exit. At the first light, turn left on Geyer Road, then left on Cragwold Road. Continue west on Cragwold Road, past the entrance to Powder Valley Conservation Nature Center, as it passes over I-270. Bear left and follow Cragwold Road about 0.6 mile further to the parking area and trail entrance.

Contact: Powder Valley Conservation Nature Center, 11715 Cragwold Road, Kirkwood 63122, 636-301-1500

ST. LOUIS

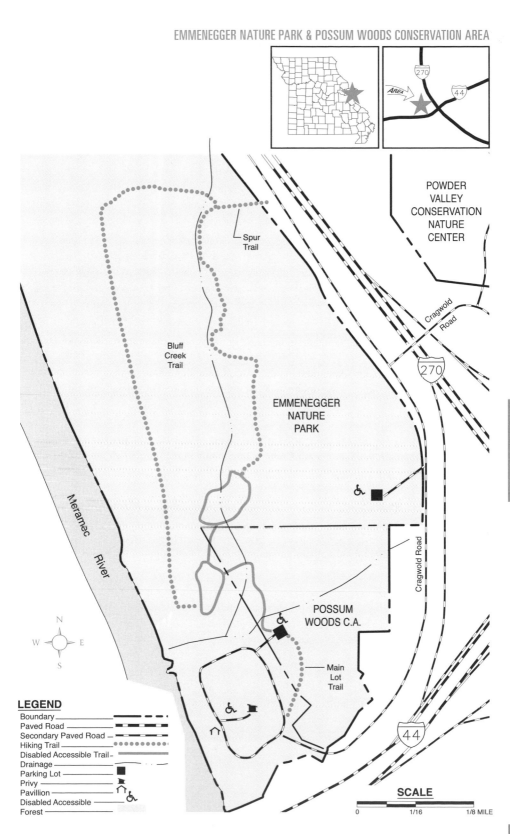

POWDER
VALLEY
CONSERVATION
NATURE
CENTER

Cragwold Road

270

Meramec River

Spur Trail

Bluff
Creek
Trail

EMMENEGGER
NATURE
PARK

ST. LOUIS

Cragwold Road

POSSUM
WOODS C.A.

Main
Lot
Trail

44

N
W E
S

LEGEND

Boundary	
Paved Road	
Secondary Paved Road	
Hiking Trail	
Disabled Accessible Trail	
Drainage	
Parking Lot	
Privy	
Pavillion	
Disabled Accessible	
Forest	

SCALE

0   1/16   1/8 MILE

49

This tract of land was once part of a large cattle ranch. Situated on the outskirts of St. Louis, Forest 44 offers a unique opportunity for urban dwellers to escape the rigors of the city and enjoy a variety of outdoor activities. In spring the area blooms with flowering dogwood and redbud. In the fall, spectacular colors light up the rugged landscape. Watch for large numbers of migrating hawks flying over the area in spring and fall. Barred owls call in the forest at sunrise and sunset, from late winter through spring. Tiger, marbled and spotted salamanders live in the moist woodland areas and around ponds. Several springs feed Williams Creek, which flows along the eastern portion of the 1,008-acre area.

The **Losing Stream Trail** begins at the south end of the parking lot. The trail gets its name from a spot where the stream disappears underground by a rock shelf, reappearing yards downstream. This asphalt, disabled-accessible trail is 0.6 mile long and has benches for resting. A viewing platform halfway along the route overlooks a small wetland demonstration area. The path crosses a spring-fed stream twice.

The **Dogwood Ridge Trail** is accessed from the west side of the Losing Stream Trail. This is a 2.2-mile double-loop, natural-surface trail. It follows a ridge back to the southern boundary of the area. You will pass two wildlife watering holes along the way. The trail then descends to the valley floor, where food plots have been planted for deer, turkey and songbirds. For a shorter hike along this trail, turn at the sign marking the short loop, a little more than a 0.25-mile up the ridge. This trail is open to foot traffic only.

A large network of **color-coded hiking and horse trails** begins west of the parking lot. Follow the path west from the parking lot and cross the stream to reach these trails, which total more than 11 miles. Trail segments weave along contours, through rich bottomland forest and along ridge tops.

Horses are allowed only on the designated multi-use trails. Bicycles are not permitted on the area.

There is a disabled-accessible privy at the main parking lot. A 20-point manned shooting range, three trap ranges, a shotgun patterning range and a field archery range are on the area's west side.

Location: From the junction of I-44 and Highway 141 in Valley Park, go south on Highway 141 to the first traffic light at Meramec Station Road. Turn right and travel 0.9 mile to Hillsboro Road, then left for 0.4 mile to the parking lot on the right.

Contact: Rockwoods Reservation, 2751 Glencoe Road, Wildwood 63038, 636-458-2236

LEGEND

Boundary	
Paved Road	
Gravel Road	
Drainage	
Wetland Demonstration Area	
Restricted Use Area	
Disabled Accessible	
Hiking Trail	
Multi-Use Trail	
Disabled Accessible Trail	
Wildlife Water Hole	
Forest	
Parking Lot	

SCALE

0   1/4   1/2 MILE

N
W — E
S

Meramec Station Rd.

Gap Gate Entrance
No Parking Area

Hillsboro Rd.

Amphibian Pond

Losing Stream Trail

Dogwood Ridge Trail

Dorothy E. Aselman
Memorial
Addition to Forest 44 C.A.

44

HUGHES MOUNTAIN NATURAL AREA

Hughes Mountain is an igneous knob named for John Hughes, the first European settler in the area. Hughes, who arrived around 1810, operated a grist mill on a creek near the mountain. The land stayed in the Hughes family until the Conservation Department purchased it in 1985.

The 462-acre area features unusual geology, glades and a variety of forest types consisting of blackjack oak, post oak, white oak, scarlet oak and black hickory. It was designated as a Missouri natural area in 1982 to protect its geology and natural communities. The Precambrian rock outcroppings on the mountain are among the oldest exposed rocks in the United States, and the rhyolite found here is approximately 1.5 billion years old. The polygonal rock formations are known locally as the Devil's Honeycomb.

Eastern red cedar has become invasive, decreasing the natural quality of the area. Consequently, restoration efforts include cedar thinning and prescribed fire. The igneous glades are dominated by little bluestem, broom sedge and poverty grass. Interesting plants include fameflower, yellow star grass, wild hyacinth and wild petunia. Lichens and mosses cling to the rocks, and prickly pear cactus grows on a few of the glade edges.

The **Devil's Honeycomb Trail** leads from the parking lot through the forest, along a steep and rocky path. At the forest edge, you are treated to your first view of the mountain. From here the trail meanders across the glade, and then veers clockwise around the summit. As the path becomes less defined, be aware of your surroundings and look back to note where you came out of the forest. Take time to wander around the glade and explore the high points for breathtaking views of the countryside. Allow at least one and a half hours for the 1.4-mile trek up to the top and back.

There are no facilities at this area, and camping is not permitted.

Location: From Potosi, travel south on Highway 21 for 11 miles to Route M. Turn east on M for 4 miles to County Road 541, then go south 0.3 mile to the parking lot on the left.

Contact: St. Louis Regional Office, 636-441-4554

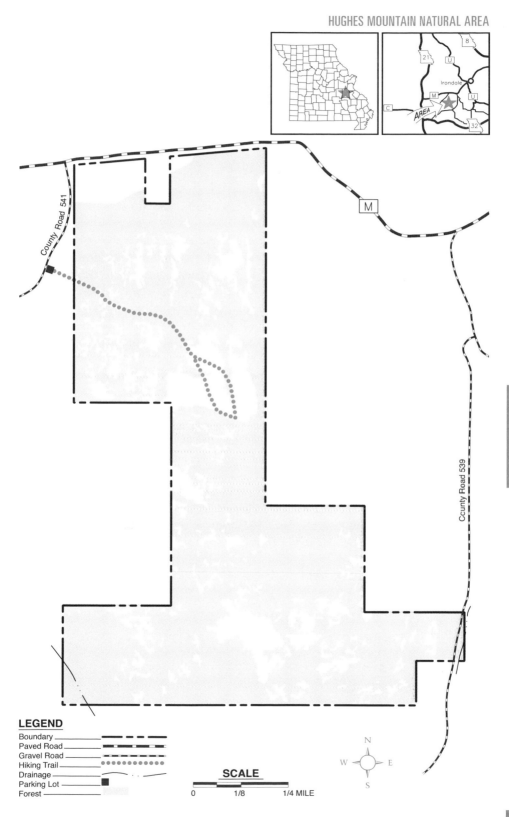

LEGEND

Boundary	
Paved Road	
Gravel Road	
Hiking Trail	
Drainage	
Parking Lot	
Forest	

SCALE

0   1/8   1/4 MILE

County Road 541

Ccunty Road 539

M

ST. LOUIS

N
W — E
S

MERAMEC CONSERVATION AREA

This 4,045-acre forested area features dolomite cliffs, pine plantations, a great blue heron rookery and abundant wildlife. Sheer cliffs along the Meramec River afford a scenic view of the river valley and surrounding hills. Interesting attractions include extensive upland forest, the old site of Reedville, the Lone Hill lookout tower site, a former Civilian Conservation Corps camp and old exploratory pits dug by early prospectors.

Visitors may choose from four trails on the area. The **Old Reedville School Trail** is a 5.5-mile natural-surface hiking trail loop. It covers a variety of terrain, from flood plain to dense oak-hickory forest, along rocky ledges and down into hollows with stream crossings. Allow three to four hours for this moderately difficult hike.

The **J. Avery Ruble Memorial Bridle Trail** consists of a large loop covering much of the area, with a shorter loop on the southern portion. This is the only area trail on which horses and bicycles are permitted. The trailhead begins near the main parking lot on the west side of the area. The trail follows an old roadbed for the first couple of miles, then heads east and north, weaving up and down across the rough terrain. The **Wet Hollow loop** is 8 miles, and the combined loop covers about 10.5 miles. The **Silver Hollow loop** is 5.5 miles. Horses and bicycles are not permitted on these trails during fall firearms deer season and spring turkey season.

The **Woodland Trail**, a 1.3-mile asphalt trail, allows people with physical disabilities to get close to nature. There are many benches along the trail route, and viewing platforms may be found near Lone Hill Onyx Cave and the Meramec River.

A **short trail** on the southwest corner of the area leads through the remains of a Civilian Conservation Corps camp established in 1934. An interpretive brochure describes the camp and some of the structures that stood nearby.

There is a disabled-accessible privy at the main parking lot. A parking lot on the east side of the area also provides access to the natural-surface trails.

Location: From Sullivan, take Highway 185 south 4.5 miles to the area entrance on the left, then follow the gravel road 1.5 miles to the main parking lot.

Contact: Sullivan Office, 375 Hwy. 185 South, Sullivan 63080, 573-468-3335

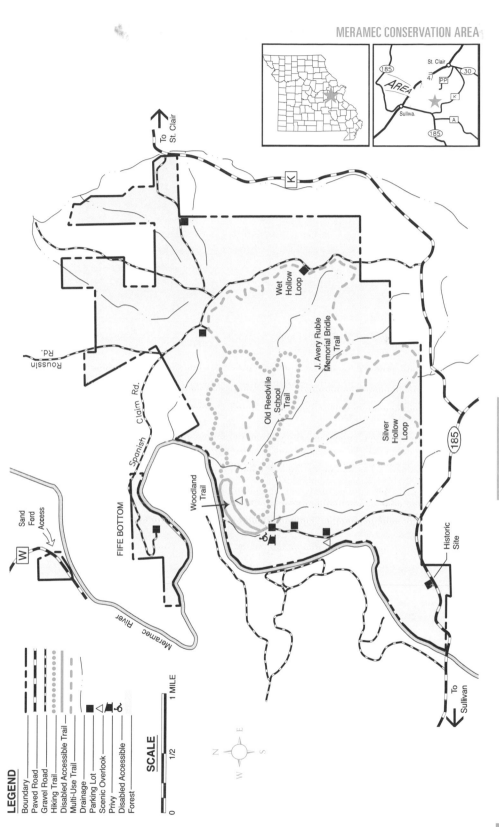

ST. LOUIS

To St. Clair

K

Roussin Rd.

Wet Hollow Loop

J. Avery Ruble Memorial Bridle Trail

Old Reedville School Trail

Silver Hollow Loop

Spanish Claim Rd.

185

Woodland Trail

FIFE BOTTOM

Sand Ford Access

W

Meramec River

Historic Site

To Sullivan

LEGEND

Boundary
Paved Road
Gravel Road
Hiking Trail
Disabled Accessible Trail
Multi-Use Trail
Drainage
Parking Lot
Scenic Overlook
Privy
Disabled Accessible
Forest

SCALE

0   1/2   1 MILE

N
E
W
S

This area west of St. Louis features 112 acres of rocky, sloping forest and intermittent streams. There is something to see in every season, from spring wildflowers to winter snow scenes. Enjoy woodland wildflowers, flowering dogwood and redbud, oak, hickory and maple trees as you walk the trails. Indoor displays in the nature center help you understand the birds, mammals, fish, reptiles and plants commonly found in Missouri backyards, parks and forests. Watch for squirrels, cottontail rabbits, raccoons, opossums, eastern chipmunks, wild turkey, woodpeckers and forest songbirds.

Visitors may hike 3 miles of paved trails through the forest. The **Tanglevine Trail** is a 0.3-mile loop beginning south of the nature center. This is the area's only disabled-accessible trail. The route curls along a wooded ridge top, where you will see some large, century-old towering white oak trees. Look for birds and hidden nests among the tangled grapevines. A fishless pond provides breeding grounds for amphibians and water for other area wildlife. Interpretive signs describe features of interest along the trail.

The **Hickory Ridge Trail** begins at the south end of the parking lot. This 1.2-mile loop has a linear connector trail that allows for a shorter loop of 0.5 mile. The trail weaves over hilltops and through a cool valley. Along the way hikers will cross seasonal creeks and pass a fishless pond. A viewing deck overlooks a seasonal stream in a wooded valley. There are approximately 2 acres of remnant savanna along the trail. Some sections of this trail are moderately steep.

The **Broken Ridge Trail** is a 0.6-mile loop beginning on the north end of the parking lot. This trail takes hikers over steep terrain and crosses a creek lined with oak, hickory and maple trees. Look for lizards on the sunlit rocky outcroppings. Visitors will notice the contrasting features of the woodlands on north- and south-facing slopes along the trail.

The nature center building includes a resource library, gift shop, four classrooms and a 250-seat auditorium used for school groups, public programs, films and guest speakers. There are two levels of exhibits, a living bee hive, and a 3,000-gallon aquarium filled with native Missouri fish. An indoor wildlife-viewing area has large windows that overlook bird feeders and a marsh, and is complete with comfortable chairs and a fireplace. Naturalist-led programs are available for organized groups.

Bicycles and jogging are not allowed on the trails. Pets are not permitted on the area, and collecting of animals, plants, fruits and mushrooms is not allowed.

Location: From the junction of I-44 and I-270 in St. Louis County, take I-44 east to the Watson Road exit. At the first light, turn left on Geyer Road, then left on Cragwold Road. Travel 0.5 mile to the entrance on the right.

Contact: Powder Valley Conservation Nature Center, 11715 Cragwold Road, Kirkwood 63122, 636-301-1500

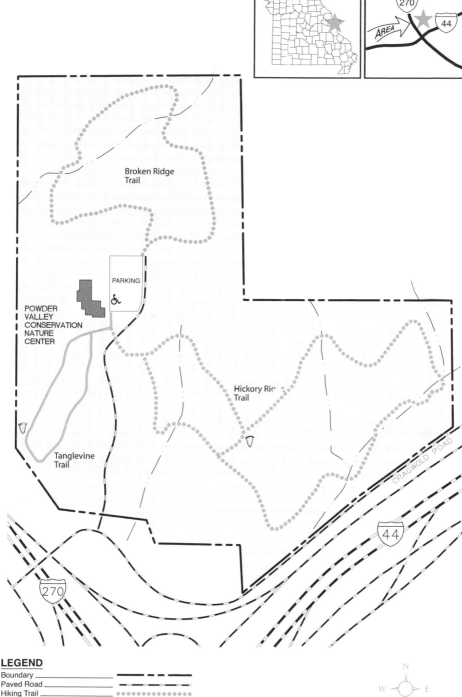

Broken Ridge Trail

PARKING

POWDER VALLEY CONSERVATION NATURE CENTER

Hickory Ridge Trail

Tanglevine Trail

CRAGWOLD ROAD

ST. LOUIS

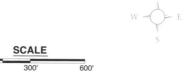

LEGEND

Boundary	
Paved Road	
Hiking Trail	
Disabled Accessible Trail	
Drainage	
Pond	◁
Forest	
Disabled Accessible	♿

N
W   E
S

SCALE

0   300'   600'

The 1,388-acre Rockwoods Range was acquired by the Conservation Department in 1943, thanks in large part to A.P. Greensfelder, who donated the land to preserve it in public ownership. Greensfelder was one of the first four people appointed to serve on the conservation commission.

This area lies in the Ozark border region, a broad transition zone where the Ozarks blend into eastern and northern regions. Ozark-like hills and hollows occur along the streams, but soils are often derived from loess (wind-blown soil) and are usually deeper and more fertile than those in the Ozarks. The ranges of many plants and animals overlap here. The area is mostly forested, but prairies, glades and other natural communities also occur. Springs, limestone rock outcrops and sinkholes are common on the area.

Scenic overlooks, tree plantations, woodland wildlife and other interesting features are found along the trails, including a memorial where a uniquely designed round house that Mr. Greensfelder built as a summer cottage once stood. The area supports good populations of deer, turkey, squirrels, raccoons, fox, rabbits and songbirds.

Hiking, biking and horseback riding opportunities are available on various trails through the area. Hikers can enjoy 2.5 miles of the **Green Rock Trail**, which continues through Greensfelder County Park and into Rockwoods Reservation. The other trails are all multi-use trails open to hiking, bicycling and horseback riding. The 3-mile **Round House Loop** trail can be reached from the east off of Allenton Road or via the 0.6-mile **Fox Creek Spur** trail, which begins at Fox Creek Road on the southern edge of the property. The **Fox Run Trail** is a 5-mile linear trail that begins at the parking lot off Fox Creek Road on the northwest corner of the conservation area.

Location: From I-44 in Allenton, take the Allenton/Six Flags exit (Exit 261) and head north on Allenton Road. Immediately turn left on Fox Creek Road and travel 1.4 miles to the parking lot on the left.

Contact: Rockwoods Reservation, 2751 Glencoe Road, Wildwood 63038, 636-458-2236

ST. LOUIS

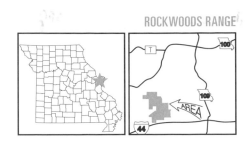

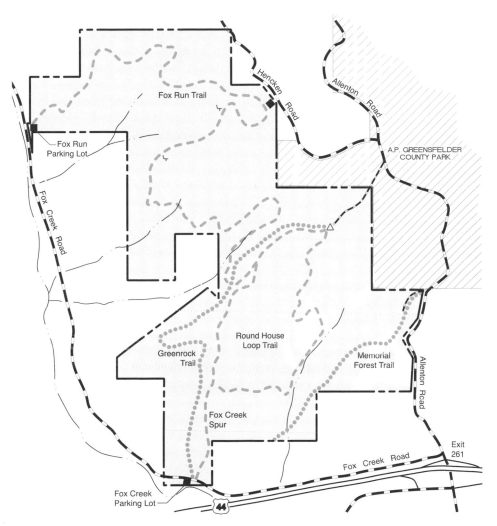

Fox Run Trail

Hencken Road

Allenton Road

A.P. GREENSFELDER
COUNTY PARK

Fox Run
Parking Lot

Fox Creek Road

ST. LOUIS

Round House
Loop Trail

Greenrock
Trail

Memorial
Forest Trail

Allenton Road

Fox Creek
Spur

Exit
261

Fox Creek Road

Fox Creek
Parking Lot

LEGEND

Boundary
Paved Road
Gravel Road
Hiking Trail
Multi-Use Trail
Drainage
Parking Lot
Scenic Rest Area
Forest
Roundhouse Memorial △

N
W E
S

SCALE

0   1/4   1/2 MILE

This 1,880-acre area is operated as a site for conservation education. It harbors not only a rich diversity of plant and animal life, but also springs, caves and rock formations. Cool, moist, north-facing ravines and lush creek bottoms contrast with the nearby arid, rocky ridge tops and south slopes. Observant visitors will be able to find remnants of extensive limestone, clay and gravel quarrying. Wildlife plantings, brush piles and invasive plant species control are used as management tools to maintain and increase the wildlife populations in the area. Interpretive signs near the education center explain special features and demonstration areas.

Visitors may choose from seven trails on the area. The **Wildlife Habitat Trail** is a 300-yard long, self-guiding loop trail. It is paved and disabled-accessible. An interpretive trail brochure provides information about various features along the route. The trailhead is on the east side of Glencoe Road, about 0.5 mile south of the education center parking lot.

The **Prairie Trail** is a 500-yard long loop trail through an experimental prairie. Along this natural-surface trail are native grasses and forbs typical of the vast prairies that once covered about one-third of the state. The parking lot and trailhead are on the east side of Glencoe Road, about 0.75 mile into the area. From this same parking lot, visitors may access the **Lime Kiln Loop Trail**. This rugged 3.2-mile natural surface loop passes by historic features that date to the late 1800s and early 1900s, when limestone mining was at its peak in the area.

The trailhead for the **Trail Among the Trees** is across the road from the north end of the education center parking lot. A self-guided, interpretive brochure is available for this 1.5-mile natural surface and asphalt trail. The brochure explains changes that have occurred in the forest throughout the years. The path ends on Glencoe Road 0.3 miles south of the trailhead. The **Rock Quarry Trail** is a 2.2-mile natural surface loop trail that winds high on the ridge behind the education center. The trailhead is near the south end of the parking lot. A linear connector trail allows for a shorter hike of about a mile. A brochure is available to help identify trees along this trail.

About 2 miles of the linear **Green Rock Trail** crosses this area. This narrow, natural surface trail has some steep and rocky portions. The trail continues southward into Greensfelder County Park, and then into Rockwoods Range, for a total length of 10 miles one-way. Parking is available at Cottonwoods Picnic Area on the west side of Glencoe Road, in Greensfelder County Park and at Rockwoods Range.

Access to the **Turkey Ridge Trail** is from a parking lot near the northeast corner of Woods Avenue and Highway 109. This 2-mile natural surface loop winds up a rocky ridge and then down a north-facing wooded slope into a shady hollow before rising back to the ridge top.

Pick up an area brochure and trail guides at the education center. Inside you will find exhibits and information about the forest, fish and wildlife resources of Missouri. Programs are available by advance registration for schools and other organized groups. There are several picnic areas along Glencoe Road, including two disabled-accessible picnic sites and an accessible restroom and drinking fountain. The education center is disabled-accessible. Camping is available to scouts and organized youth groups by reservation only. Pets are not permitted on this area.

Location: From I-44 in Eureka, take Highway 109 north about 3.5 miles to the conservation area sign at Woods Road. Turn left, then right on Glencoe Road and travel 1.5 miles to the education center on the left.

Contact: Rockwoods Reservation, 2751 Glencoe Road, Wildwood 63038, 636-458-2236

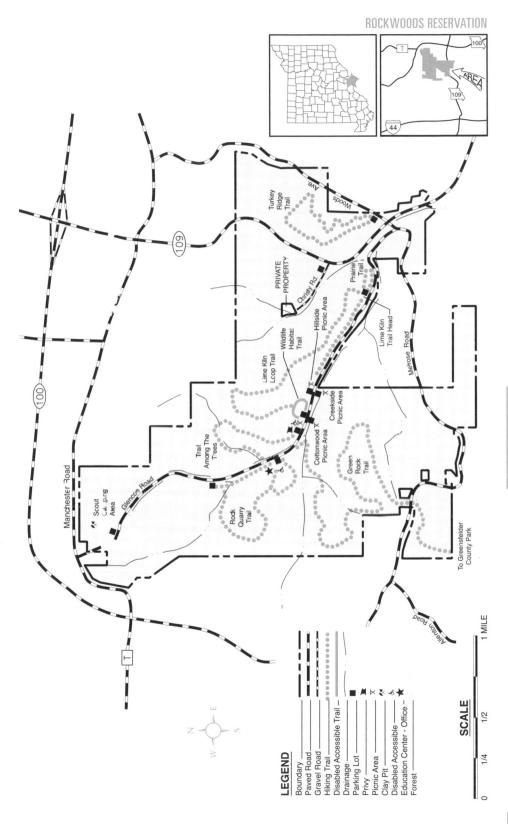

ST. LOUIS

LEGEND
Boundary
Paved Road
Gravel Road
Hiking Trail
Disabled Accessible Trail
Drainage
Parking Lot
Privy
Picnic Area
Disabled Accessible
Education Center - Office
Forest

SCALE
0   1/4   1/2   1 MILE

Turkey Ridge Trail

Woods Ave.

PRIVATE PROPERTY

Christy Rd.

Prairie Trail

Wildlife Habitat Trail

Hillside Picnic Area

Lime Kiln Loop Trail

Lime Kiln Trail Head

Melrose Road

Creekside Picnic Area

Cottonwood Picnic Area

Green Rock Trail

Trail Among The Trees

Rock Quarry Trail

Glencoe Road

Scout Camping Area

Manchester Road

To Greensfelder County Park

Allenton Road

109

100

T

44

109

100

AREA

N
E
S
W

✳VALLEY VIEW GLADES NATURAL AREA

This scenic 225-acre area in central Jefferson County is part of a large glade complex. The glades are dominated by little bluestem, big bluestem, Indian grass and prairie dropseed. Fremont's leather flower, prairie turnip and Missouri evening primrose are a few of the interesting glade plants. Butterfly weed and black-eyed Susan bloom in early summer, attracting glade grasshoppers and many species of butterflies. You may see grassland songbirds such as prairie warblers, field sparrows and red-eyed vireos. Watch for six-lined racerunners and fence and eastern collared lizards sunning on rocks.

The 2.5-mile **Valley View Glades Trail** loops through scenic glades, sheltered valleys, along wooded ridges and open rocky slopes of prairie grass. From the parking lot, a short path leads downhill through forest, then suddenly emerges on the glades. Stop at this point and take in the great views. Directly in front of you the terrain drops away to a tree-lined ravine and rises across another glade expanse, with forest in the distance. At the halfway point of your hike you will be on the opposite side of the area, looking back to where you now stand. Begin the loop by heading left across the glade and into the forest. You will weave across streams and along the western and then northern area boundary where the trail reaches its highest point. It follows an old roadbed along the ridge for a distance, then curves south and heads down through the grasses, into forest again, and to the final stream crossing. The trail winds uphill through grass and back to the glade where you began.

The glades are mixed with small pockets of dry, upland forest dominated by blackjack oak. Other trees and shrubs found on the glades include eastern red cedar, post oak, flowering dogwood and fragrant sumac. Thin, rocky soil here produces dwarfed, often short-lived trees. The rock is dolomite, a dark limestone containing magnesium. Small intermittent streams drain the glades and add to the area's diversity. Even though it is a small area, there are remarkable examples of stream ledges, waterfalls, overhangs and pools.

The foot path is signed in a clockwise direction, but is not well worn, so keep an eye out for the trail signs. Allow two to three hours for the moderately difficult hike. Bicycles and horses are not permitted on the area. There are no facilities here, and camping is not permitted. Destroying, cutting or removing vegetation is prohibited. The taking of wild greens from natural areas is not allowed. A number of small animals require natural shelters provided by flat rocks; please do not turn over any rocks on this property.

Location: From the intersection of Highway 21 and Route B in Hillsboro, go west on Route B for 4.5 miles to the parking area on the right side of the road.

Contact: Rockwoods Reservation, 2751 Glencoe Road, Wildwood 63038, 636-458-2236

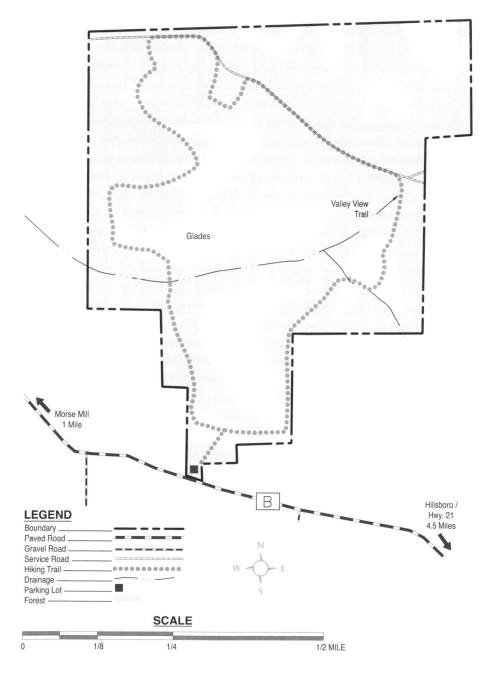

Valley View Trail

Glades

Morse Mill
1 Mile

Hillsboro /
Hwy. 21
4.5 Miles

B

LEGEND

Boundary	
Paved Road	
Gravel Road	
Service Road	
Hiking Trail	
Drainage	
Parking Lot	■
Forest	

N
W E
S

ST. LOUIS

SCALE

0   1/8   1/4   1/2 MILE

As with Valley View Glades, the Victoria Glades are part of a large complex of glades starting just east of the Big River near Morse Mill and extending eastward, beyond Hillsboro and Desoto, to Festus and then south into Ste. Genevieve County. This large complex of glades occur in a band 2- to 5-miles wide. Glades within the 239-acre conservation area are principally on Jefferson City-Cotter dolomite of Ordivician age. A similar concentration of glades occurs in southern Missouri in the White River Hills region.

The Jefferson County glades are commonly found on south and southwest-facing slopes with forested ridges and are characterized by thin soil and bedrock at or near the surface. Water saturates the ground in winter and spring, but soils become droughty in summer and fall. Grasses and broad-leaved, flowering plants are plentiful. Little bluestem, Indian grass, side oats grama, big bluestem and prairie dropseed are common grasses. Scores of non-grass species provide food for wildlife and add beautiful color to the glades during seasonal peaks.

Small pockets of dry upland forest dominated by blackjack oak also are established here. Other trees and shrubs found on the glades include eastern red cedar, gum bumelia, post oak, flowering dogwood, Indian cherry and fragrant sumac. Forest vegetation surrounds the open glade areas. Many kinds of snakes and lizards as well as larger animals, such as deer and turkey, live in this area.

The **Victoria Glades Trail** is a marked loop that runs 2.3 miles through the oak/hickory forest and partly on the glade. From the parking lot, cross the road to the trailhead that leads uphill immediately onto the glade. Follow the path to the right as it enters the forest. The rocky trail weaves along the northern area boundary, then curves south and returns along the southern area boundary. At this point you'll leave the forest and head back through the glade to the starting point. Be careful here and look ahead for trail markers as the path across the glade may not be obvious. Allow two hours for the hike and glade exploration.

Bicycles and horses are not permitted on the area, and camping is not allowed. Destroying, cutting or removing vegetation is prohibited. Taking of wild greens from natural areas is not allowed.

Location: At the junction of Highway 21 and Route BB in Hillsboro, head east on BB (Main Street). Turn right on Vreeland Road, which changes to Victoria-Hillsboro Road, and travel 1.7 miles to the parking area on the left. Cross the road to enter the conservation area.

Contact: Rockwoods Reservation, 2751 Glencoe Road, Wildwood 63038, 636-458-2236

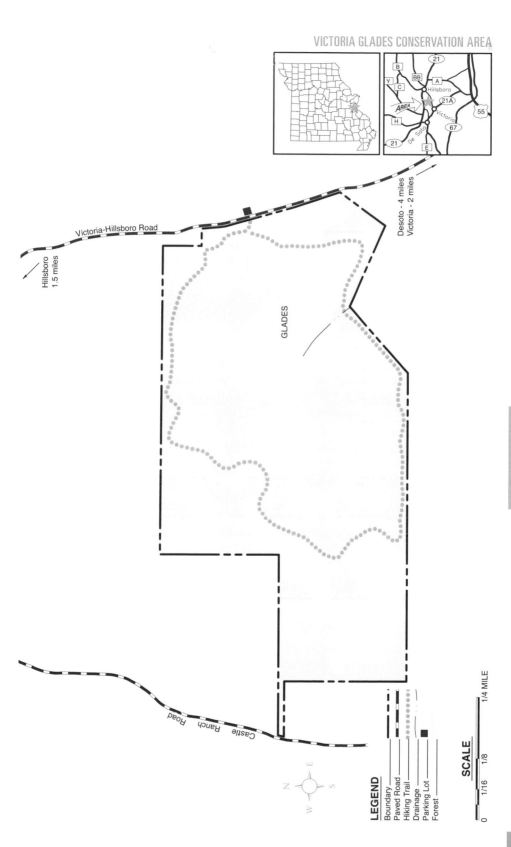

ST. LOUIS

GLADES

Victoria-Hillsboro Road

Hillsboro
1.5 miles

Desoto - 4 miles
Victoria - 2 miles

Castle Ranch Road

21
B
Y
C
BB
A
Hillsboro
21A
AREA
De Soto
Victoria
55
67
H
21
E

N
W · E
S

LEGEND
Boundary
Paved Road
Hiking Trail
Drainage
Parking Lot
Forest

SCALE
0   1/16   1/8   1/4 MILE

Located in St. Charles County, this area is named after John Weldon, who came to the region in 1796 with a Spanish Land Grant for 425 acres. During World War II, the federal government acquired almost 17,000 acres in the area for the construction of a munitions plant. In 1948 all of the property except the munitions plant was given to the University of Missouri for an agricultural experiment station. The Conservation Department purchased more than 7,000 acres from the university in 1978.

Hiking and biking opportunities abound on Weldon Spring Conservation Area. The 8.2-mile **Lewis Trail** weaves through scenic upland and bottomland forest and across intermittent streams. A portion of this trail follows along the high bluff above the Missouri River. The **Clark Trail** is a 5.3-mile loop contained within the Lewis Trail. Portions of the Lewis and Clark Trails are in the Weldon Spring Hollow Natural Area, where natural features include limestone cliffs and bluff escarpments. Wildflowers are abundant on the natural area in the spring. Along the trails you may see columbine, cliffbrake fern and more unusual plants such as the three-bird orchid, the late coral root orchid and a 39-inch diameter bitternut hickory. The Lewis Trail and the Clark Trail are open to hiking only. Allow about three hours for the Clark Trail loop, and five hours for the Lewis Trail.

Two connected loops form the 10-mile **Lost Valley Hiking & Biking Trail** on the west half of the area. This trail runs parallel to branches of Little Femme Osage Creek, and passes a spring-fed beaver pond. Part of the trail is along an old road bed while forested sections are somewhat narrow and steep. The 8-mile gravel-surfaced **Hamburg Trail** winds through Weldon Spring Conservation Area adjacent to Highway 94, and connects the nearby August A. Busch Memorial Conservation Area to the **Katy Trail**. Managed by the Department of Natural Resources, Katy Trail State Park passes through the southern portion of Weldon Spring Conservation Area and parallels the Missouri River for 5.3 miles. Bicycles are permitted on the natural-surface Lost Valley Hiking & Biking Trail, the Hamburg Trail and the Katy Trail.

Location: From Highway 40/61 at Weldon Spring, travel west on Highway 94, past Highway D (turn right at Highway D to visit the August A. Busch Memorial Conservation Area). To hike the Lewis and Clark Trails, follow Highway 94 for 1.1 mile past Highway D and turn left into the parking lot. The next two parking lots on the right side of Highway 94 provide access to the Hamburg Trail. Parking for the Lost Valley Trail is on the right at the bottom of the hill, about 5.5 miles from Highway D.

Contact: St. Louis Regional Office, 636-441-4554

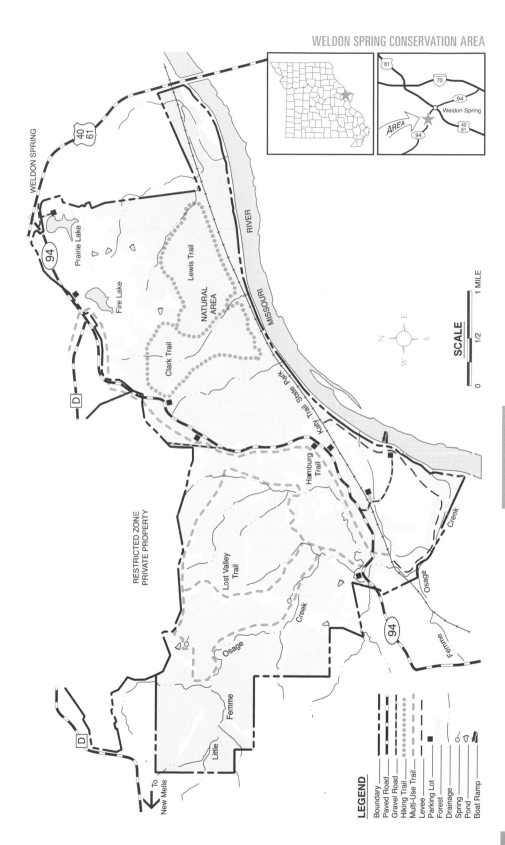

WELDON SPRING CONSERVATION AREA

ST. LOUIS

SCALE

0   1/2   1 MILE

MISSOURI RIVER

Prairie Lake

Fire Lake

Lewis Trail

NATURAL AREA

Clark Trail

Katy Trail State Park

Hamburg Trail

RESTRICTED ZONE
PRIVATE PROPERTY

Lost Valley Trail

Osage Creek

Osage Creek

Femme Osage Creek

Little Femme

WELDON SPRING

To
New Melle

Weldon Spring

AREA

LEGEND

Boundary
Paved Road
Gravel Road
Hiking Trail
Multi-Use Trail
Levee
Parking Lot
Forest
Drainage
Spring
Pond
Boat Ramp

BUSIEK STATE FOREST AND WILDLIFE AREA

The Conservation Department purchased the original tract of land for the Busiek area in 1981 and additional purchases have brought the area to its present 2,502-acre size. More than 90 percent of the area is forested. Woods Fork of Bull Creek flows across 2.5 miles of the area, and Camp Creek flows 2.5 miles to its confluence with Woods Fork. The topography of the area is typical of the Ozark plateau, with steep, rocky hills and gravel-bottom creeks. Some of the steeper south and west facing slopes have developed into glades. Prairie dock, compass plant, larkspur and Indian paintbrush are common on these open areas.

The area is managed primarily for outdoor recreation, education and wildlife habitat improvement. Forest management techniques including limited timber harvest are used to improve tree growth and quality, and increase wildlife habitat diversity. Several old home sites, none of historical significance, can be found on the area. The Carter family cemetery is located on the ridge above the confluence of Woods Fork and Camp Creek, with headstones dating back to the 1800s.

More than 18 miles of **multi-use trails** cover the area's east and west sides. All trail routes are marked with colored blazes on trees. "You are here" signs are posted at various intersections to help trail users navigate the different loops. Most of the trails have a rough and rocky surface, so sturdy hiking boots are recommended. A couple of trails have shorter connector routes that bypass some of the steep terrain. Hikers should be prepared for multiple creek crossings and the probability of getting wet feet during much of the year. However, in late summer the creeks are low enough that crossing can be accomplished without encountering water. Two new bridges are being added, and these will provide increased access to much of the trail system.

All designated trails are open to hiking, bicycling and horseback riding. Primitive camping on a walk-in basis is allowed. Campers must obtain a special-use permit prior to their visit. Campsites must be at least 100 yards from all public access roads, trails and parking lots. An unattended public shooting range is located on the area.

Location: From the junction of Highways 60 and 65 in south Springfield, travel south on Highway 65 for 18 miles to the conservation area sign and entrance on the left. Follow the entrance road to the T-intersection and turn left to access trails on the east side of the area. Pass the large equestrian parking lot and continue to the smaller parking area and trailheads. To access trails on the west side of the area, turn right at the T-intersection and travel to the parking area at the end of the road.

Contact: Southwest Regional Office, 417-895-6880

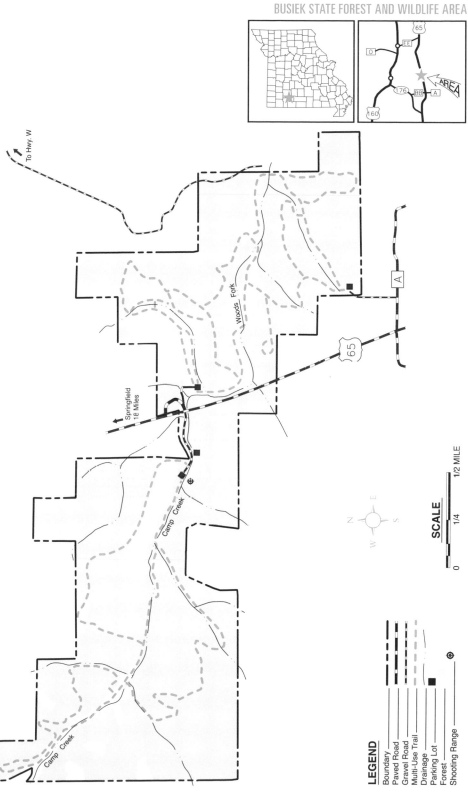

SOUTHWEST

✛ COMPTON HOLLOW CONSERVATION AREA

Compton Hollow Conservation Area contains three distinct natural features: a post oak flatwoods, several small dolomite glades and a dry-mesic chert forest. These features are protected and managed to maintain or increase their natural qualities. Approximately 90 percent of this area is forested. Non-forested areas are composed of old fields and wildlife food plots. Several small ponds provide wildlife watering holes. The area is home to numerous game and nongame species, including deer, turkey, squirrel and raccoon. Food plots, forest thinnings and small forest clearings are designed to improve wildlife habitat. Other management projects include prescribed burnings in some of the old fields, and edge feathering along the fields to enhance quail habitat.

A 5.5 mile **multi-use trail system** covers most of the area. These trails are open to hiking, bicycling and horseback riding and provide variety for all experience levels. From the parking lot on the northwest corner of the area, a wide gravel trail leads across the central portion of the area. Some connecting trail segments follow a natural surface two-track road, while other portions are a narrower single-track trail, covering rocky steep terrain.

Visitors should be aware of hunters in the fall. Primitive camping on a walk-in basis is allowed. Campsites must be at least 100 yards from all public access roads, open fields and parking lots. An archery field course is located near the east parking lot. There are no facilities on the area.

Location: From Springfield, take I-44 east to Route B (Exit 96). Travel south for 4.2 miles to Conservation Lane on the left. Follow this road 0.3 miles south to the small parking area on the left. To reach larger parking areas that can accommodate horse trailers, travel further south on Route B and turn left on Compton Hollow Road.

Contact: Southwest Regional Office, 417-895-6880

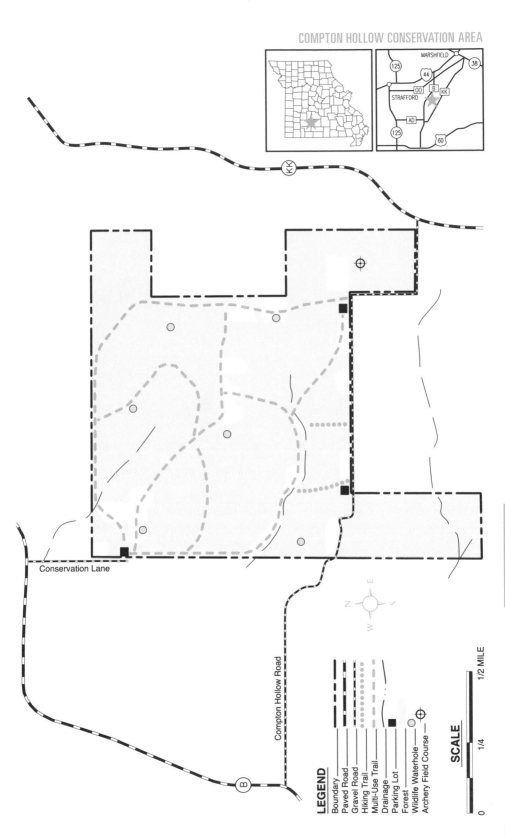

MARSHFIELD

STRAFFORD

Conservation Lane

Compton Hollow Road

SOUTHWEST

LEGEND
Boundary
Paved Road
Gravel Road
Hiking Trail
Multi-Use Trail
Drainage
Parking Lot
Forest
Wildlife Waterhole
Archery Field Course

SCALE

0   1/4   1/2 MILE

Steep hills covered in oak-hickory forest constitute much of the 1,534-acre Henning Conservation Area, which lies in the White River hills west of Branson. The forest is broken by a series of limestone and dolomite glades that compose the White River Balds Natural Area. The natural area is home to the uncommon smoke tree and Ashe juniper, as well as beautiful glade wildflowers. Many reptiles, tarantulas and scorpions also live here. The glades or "balds" played an important role in the history and folklore of the region. According to legend, the balds became gathering spots for local vigilantes after the Civil War. The "baldknobbers," as they were called, would meet on the glades to plan their escapades.

Three hiking trails on the south side of the area allow for both forest and glade exploration. At the south end of the parking lot is the trailhead for the **Dewey Bald Trail**. This 0.4-mile asphalt trail is paved, but is not disabled-accessible. It winds to the top of Dewey Bald, where you may climb a 40-foot tower for sweeping views of the scenic White River hills and the City of Branson.

The **Glade Trail** loop begins from a covered deck at the north end of the main parking lot. Look for fence and eastern collared lizards sunning themselves on rocky outcrops along the trail. A hike of 0.7 mile along this path leads to an overlook deck in the natural area. From here you may look across to Cox's Bald and South Cox's Bald, and down into Dewey Cove. Past the overlook, the trail loops down through the glade and back to the parking lot on Cedar Bald, a 1.1-mile trip. For a longer hike, cross over to the **Streamside Trail** where it connects with the Glade Trail. Walking both the loops takes about an hour and covers 1.5 miles. A brochure with a map of the trails is available at the trailhead.

For a longer, more rugged hike, try the **Henning Homesteaders Trail**. Access to the trail is from **Shane's Shortcut** on the east side of the Streamside Trail, or by driving to a small parking area on the north side of the conservation area. This 3.4-mile natural-surface loop trail is moderately steep and rough in spots, so allow about three hours to hike. The trail was built by a Boy Scout troop and is marked by blaze orange on the trees. From the north parking lot, the trail begins along Roark Creek, a relatively undisturbed Ozark headwaters stream. A self-guided trail booklet is available to describe some of the natural features and historical sites you will encounter along the route. These include a number of old home sites from the late 1800s. Send for the trail booklet, or pick one up at the Springfield Conservation Nature Center, Shepherd of the Hills Fish Hatchery, Branson Forestry Office or on site from a brochure box at the trailhead.

Full-color interpretive signs are displayed along the rock wall at the main parking area's scenic overlook. They provide general area information and describe why glades are special Ozark habitats. A privy is located near the main parking lot. Camping is not permitted.

Location: To reach the Scenic Overlook, Dewey Bald and Glade Trails from the junction of Highway 65 and Highway 465 5 miles north of Branson, take Highway 465 (Ozark Mountain High Road) west for 7 miles to Highway 76. At Highway 76 go east for 2 miles to the area entrance on the left.

To reach the Homesteaders Trail from the junction of Highways 65 and 465, travel west on Highway 465 for 2 miles. Take the Highway 248 exit and turn left. After 0.25 mile, turn right on Road 248-20 (Sycamore Log Church Road). Drive 3.7 miles to the parking lot on the left. The trailhead is just across the low water bridge on Roark Creek.

Contact: Southwest Regional Office, 417-895-6880

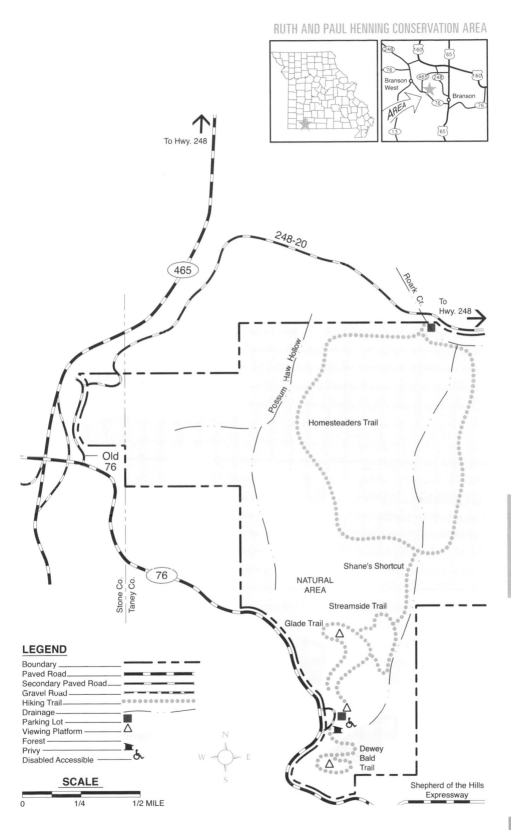

To Hwy. 248

465

248-20

Roark Cr.

To Hwy. 248

Possum Haw Hollow

Homesteaders Trail

SOUTHWEST

Old 76

Shane's Shortcut

NATURAL AREA

Streamside Trail

Stone Co.
Taney Co.

76

Glade Trail

Dewey Bald Trail

Shepherd of the Hills Expressway

LEGEND

Boundary	
Paved Road	
Secondary Paved Road	
Gravel Road	
Hiking Trail	
Drainage	
Parking Lot	■
Viewing Platform	△
Forest	
Privy	
Disabled Accessible	♿

N
W — E
S

SCALE

0   1/4   1/2 MILE

Pilot Knob Conservation Area is a 1,360-acre tract that was acquired in 1998 by a land exchange with the U.S. Forest Service. The name Pilot Knob comes from the use of the tall hilltops in the Ozarks as reference and triangulation points. The tops of the highest hills were often cleared of all but one tall tree. This "signal tree" designated the hilltop as a pilot knob. At the turn of the 20th century, several pilot knobs existed in southwest Missouri. Legend has it that Native Americans and baldknobbers used the knobs for various activities. Today, many of these hilltops have re-grown with vegetation, but some remain bald.

Much of this conservation area consists of steep hills covered with typical upland oak-hickory forest. Within the forest are glades—open, rocky areas on south and west facing slopes. On the glades are native warm season grasses, coneflowers, prickly pear cactus and lizards.

The 2.7-mile **Ridge Top Trail** begins at the Highway 39 parking lot and ends at an old woods road near the northeast corner of the conservation area. From the parking lot, hikers will begin an uphill climb on a wide, rocky path. For a short distance the trail follows a power line corridor, then turns back into the forest. Notice the rock ledges on the higher slope to the right of the trail, and the view of distant hills from the opposite side of the trail.

The middle portion of the trail is mostly level as it follows a ridgeline through the area. Near the end of the trail, an unmaintained woods road leads to the top of the pilot knob. Allow three hours to hike to the far end of the Ridge Top Trail and back to the parking area.

Location: Pilot Knob Conservation Area is in the far southwest corner of Stone County. From the junction of Highways 39 and 86 at the town of Carr Lane, travel north on Highway 39 for approximately 3 miles to the parking area on the east side of the road.

Contact: Southwest Regional Office, 417-895-6880

SOUTHWEST

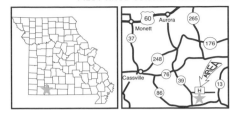

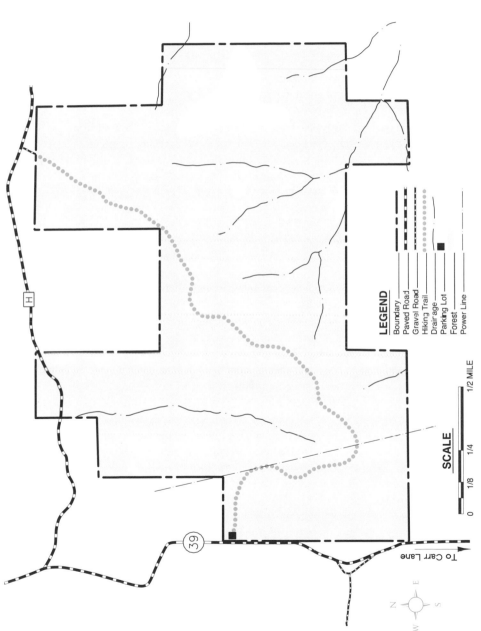

LEGEND
Boundary
Paved Road
Gravel Road
Hiking Trail
Drainage
Parking Lot
Forest
Power Line

SCALE
0   1/8   1/4   1/2 MILE

To Carr Lane

39

H

SOUTHWEST

75

✛ SPRINGFIELD CONSERVATION NATURE CENTER

This 80-acre area features both upland and bottomland forests, a small restored savanna, a bottomland prairie planting, a 5-acre glade, creek frontage, marshy wetlands, karst topography including a losing stream and a small spring, and frontage on Lake Springfield. Visitors often are treated to close-up views of the area's healthy population of white-tailed deer and wild turkeys. Gray squirrels and chipmunks are common sights along the wooded trails, while muskrat, mink, turtles and frogs may be seen in the wetland areas. The diverse habitat attracts a wide variety of birds; more than 174 species have been recorded on the property. Spring warbler migration is at its peak during the second week in May.

Visitors have the opportunity to experience a variety of natural communities on nearly 3 miles of connected trails. The **Savanna Ridge trail** is a 0.2-mile loop beginning at the trailhead northeast of the nature center building. It passes through a restored savanna with sprawling white oak trees and an understory of prairie grasses and forbs. This trail is paved, but does not meet accessibility standards for the disabled.

The 0.3-mile paved **Boardwalk Trail** has a steep slope. Access the trail from the trailhead or from the east exit of the nature center building. An observation deck provides views into the understory of a typical Ozark forest. Continue along a contour of the hill into a valley, and turn left at the bridge to stay on the Boardwalk Trail. The loop portion includes a wooden boardwalk over the marshy shallows of Lake Springfield. Watch for green frogs and common, harmless water snakes along the water's edge. Cattails provide the perfect spot to see red-winged blackbirds and an occasional muskrat. Look for signs of beaver activity in this area.

The 1.7 mile **Long Trail** begins at the north end of the Savanna Ridge loop. It winds down a slope, along Galloway Creek, and across two bridges. The path then leads through a bottomland prairie planting and turns west to cross a long bridge over an arm of Lake Springfield. This is a good spot to see fish and turtles. Just before the bridge is the 0.1-mile **Photo Blind Trail**, a linear path that leads to a photo blind on the lake. For additional hiking opportunity, take a left turn shortly after the second bridge on the Long Trail. Here, a connector trail leads outside of nature center property to the **Galloway Creek Greenway**, a 5-mile trail segment managed by Ozark Greenways Inc.

Across the bridge over Lake Springfield, a right turn leads back to the Boardwalk Trail and the nature center via the 0.1-mile **Sycamore Cut-off Trail**. Or turn left after the bridge to continue on Long Trail. This section passes by a small spring and a losing stream before meandering through a glade, where you may see prickly pear cactus and basking lizards.

The **Fox Bluff Trail** forms a 0.3-mile loop, with a linear section connecting to the Boardwalk Trail. Benches at two sites along the trail beckon hikers to stop and enjoy scenic overviews of Lake Springfield. Spring wildflowers are abundant along the wooded slopes here. Spicebush, a common fragrant shrub, grows along both sides of the path that leads downhill to connect with the Boardwalk Trail.

Facilities inside the nature center include exhibits, two classrooms, a 150-seat auditorium, a wildlife viewing area, gift shop and restrooms. The center has regularly scheduled public programs, nature films and guided walks. A covered pavilion with restrooms is next to the nature center building. Pets, hunting, fishing and collecting are not permitted on the grounds.

Location: The Springfield Conservation Nature Center is in southeast Springfield just west of Highway 65 off the James River Freeway (Highway 60). Follow brown directional signs to the nature center.

Contact: Springfield Conservation Nature Center, 4600 S. Chrisman, Springfield 65804, 417-888-4237

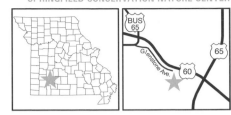

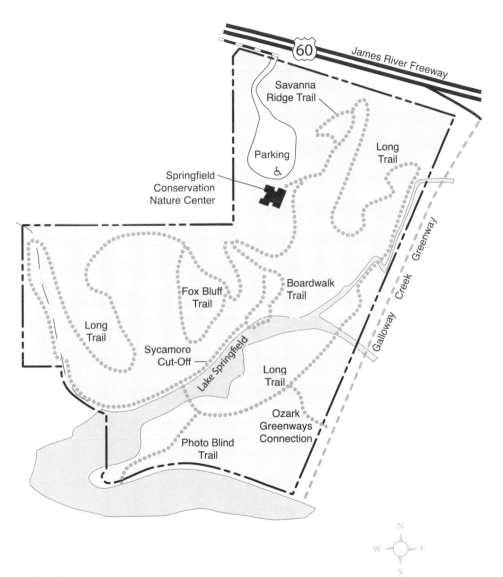

SOUTHWEST

LEGEND

Boundary	
Paved Road	
Drainage	
Hiking Trail	
Multi-Use Trail	
Forest	
Disabled Accessible	&#9855;

SCALE

0   1/16   1/8   1/4 MILE

✳ ANGELINE CONSERVATION AREA

This 39,000-acre forested area, just north of Eminence, is a showcase of Missouri's trees. Species include white, post and black oak, hickory, eastern red cedar, and shortleaf pine—Missouri's only native pine. Our state tree, the flowering dogwood, is abundant and comes into full bloom in early spring. Soils here vary from relatively deep to thin and gladelike. A variety of lichens and mosses adorn the rocks and trees. One of the highlights of the area is the shut-ins through Lick Log Hollow. The action of water moving through fast-eroding limestone has worn the rock down to a lower stratum of more resistant rhyolite, creating this natural scenic feature.

The **Lick Log Hollow Nature Trail** is a 1-mile loop around a creek that flows through the hollow. The gravel trail is wide and mostly level, allowing for an easy walk. It winds through a small portion of the area, through forest and glade, across streams and past old fields where crops grew many years ago. A connector trail midway along the route allows for a shorter hike. A self-guided trail brochure has interpretive references corresponding to numbered posts along the route. It also provides descriptions of several tree species found along the trail.

In the forest, look for differences in tree growth; the taller trees are in deeper soils, the shorter trees are in relatively thin soils. Along the trail you will see dead trees, both standing and lying on the ground. These trees provide insects for birds and a home for cavity-nesting birds and animals.

Self-guided trail brochures are available at the Eminence Conservation Department office. There are no facilities at the trail parking lot. Primitive camping is allowed.

Location: From Eminence, head north on Highway 19. Just past the Conservation Department office is a scenic overlook, and about 0.8 mile farther north is Foxpen Road. Turn right and follow the gravel road 0.3 mile to the area entrance on the right.

Contact: Eminence Office, P.O. Box 755, Eminence 65466, 573-226-3616

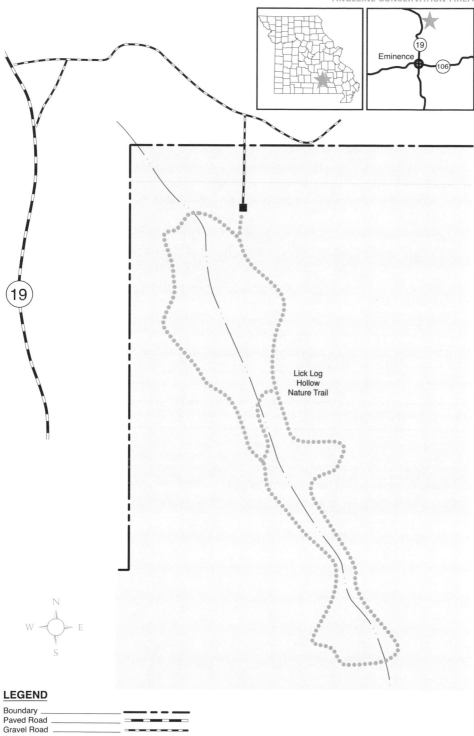

Eminence

19

106

Lick Log
Hollow
Nature Trail

19

N
W · E
S

OZARK

LEGEND

Boundary
Paved Road
Gravel Road
Drainage
Hiking Trail
Forest
Parking Lot

SCALE

0   1/16   1/8   1/4 MILE

TINGLER PRAIRIE CONSERVATION AREA

Tingler Prairie is the only known high-quality remaining tallgrass prairie on public land in the lower Missouri Ozarks. The area's prairies, woodlands and bottomland forest comprise 240 acres and are home to more than 400 species of plants and animals.

From the parking lot, visitors have a choice of walking one, two or all three of the area's interconnected trails. The **Sinkhole Pond Trail** is an easy 0.5-mile walk around a large sinkhole pond basin. Sinkholes are formed when the roof of a cave below ground collapses or when underlying rock is slowly dissolved by water. The pond is home to numerous rare plants as well as over a dozen dragonfly species. An overlook allows hikers to get a good view of the sinkhole and is a great place to sit and listen to the calls of the many frog and toad species that inhabit the pond in early and late summer.

The **Woodland Trail** is a 0.5-mile loop through 80 acres of Ozark woodland and along the South Fork of Spring Creek. Most of the trees in the dry woodlands here are from the oak and hickory families. The trail offers opportunities to view a variety of wildlife including song birds, turtles, deer, and along the creek, the occasional muskrat and beaver.

On the 1-mile **Prairie Trail**, visitors can travel back to a time when the southern Missouri Ozarks were dotted with native prairies. During summer, native grasses can be up to 8 feet tall and wildflowers are in full bloom throughout the prairie. Prairie plants have deep roots, which help trap sediments and pollutants; consequently they help protect water quality. Expect to see numerous song birds including eastern meadowlark, dickcissel, eastern peewee, chipping sparrow and grasshopper sparrow.

Location: From West Plains follow Highway 17 south approximately 6 miles to County Road 910. Travel west to County Road 811, then go south 0.3 mile to the area parking lot.

Contact: Ozark Regional Office, 417-256-7161

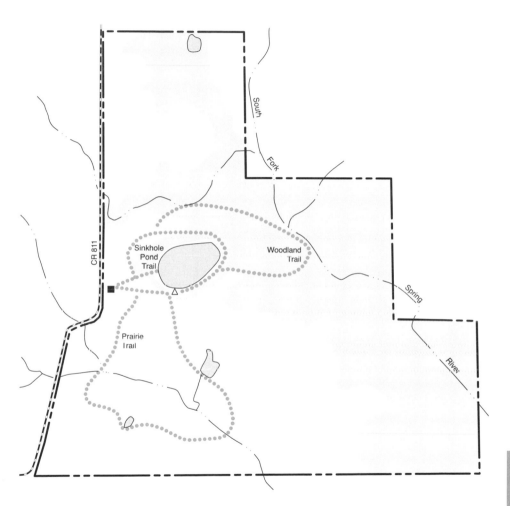

OZARK

LEGEND

Boundary	
Gravel Road	
Hiking Trail	
Drainage	
Parking Lot	■
Forest	
Overlook	△
Pond	⬭

N
W — E
S

SCALE

0	1/8	1/4 MILE

On the upper reaches of the Castor River in Bollinger and Madison counties, this historic 1,632-acre area is locally known as Hahns Mill. In the late 1800s two brothers operated grain mills here. A 282-acre area has been designated as the Castor River Shut-ins Natural Area. This is one of the few granite shut-ins in Missouri. Throughout thousands of years, the clear waters of the Castor River have carved the ancient pink rock to create deep, gorgelike chutes. Shortleaf pines and cedars dot the steep river banks, with mixed oaks, hickory, sugar maple, white ash, blackgum, sassafras and persimmon in the adjacent forest.

Interesting species found on Amidon's glades include pineweed, wild hyacinth, prickly pear cactus and fame flower. The glades are being restored through cedar removal and prescribed fire. The result of this management is increased light, which encourages native grasses and wildflowers. Watering ponds have been created and food plots and crop fields planted to provide additional wildlife food sources. Occasional timber harvests produce forage and cover for wildlife.

The 1-mile **Cedar Glade Trail** is a natural-surface path through varied terrain. It begins at the edge of a field and weaves through thick forest cover, suddenly emerging on huge granite rocks that line the edge of the river. You will hear the water rushing through the shut-ins before you are able to see them. Walk out among the rocks and explore, but pay attention to the trail signs so that you can pick up the path again farther along the rocks to the south. Here the trail veers to the right and climbs a slope, leveling out across a glade area. If you miss the turn you'll find yourself following a dirt path downhill to a calmer section of river. From the glade, the hiking trail descends back into the forest and along a dry hollow. It will take about 30 minutes to hike the entire loop, but plan to spend time exploring along the rocks and the river.

Primitive camping in designated areas is permitted from Oct. 1 to Dec. 31. There are no facilities at this area.

Location: From Fredericktown, take Highway 72 east, continue east on Route J for 4 miles, then south on Route W for 1.3 miles until the pavement ends at County Road 208. Turn left on 208, then left on County Road 253 for 0.9 mile to the parking lot on the right.

Contact: Southeast Regional Office, 573-290-5730

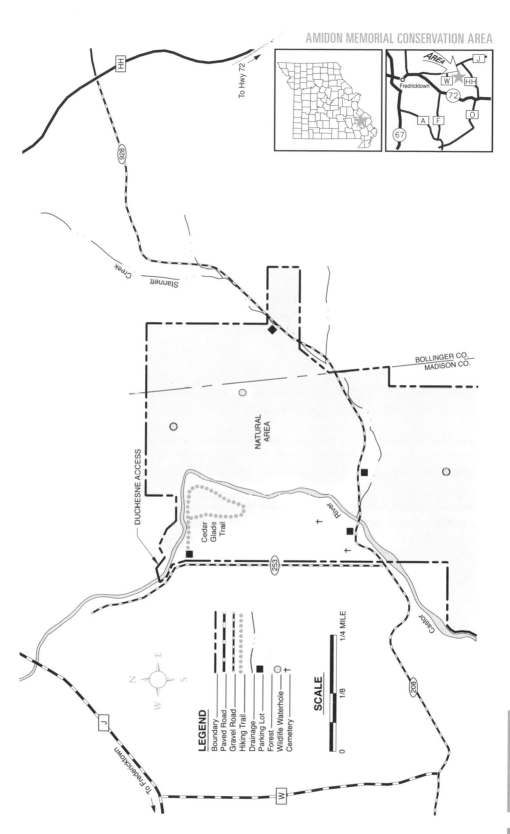

AREA

Fredricktown

To Hwy 72

HH

928

Stannett Creek

BOLLINGER CO.
MADISON CO.

DUCHESNE ACCESS

NATURAL
AREA

Cedar
Glade
Trail

River

253

Castor

208

To Fredricktown

J

W

LEGEND
Boundary
Paved Road
Gravel Road
Hiking Trail
Drainage
Parking Lot
Forest
Wildlife Waterhole
Cemetery

N
E
S
W

SCALE

0   1/8   1/4 MILE

On the grounds of North Cape County Park and next door to the Southeast Regional Office, you'll find the Conservation Department's newest nature center. The area features an oak-hickory forest, marsh and pond habitats, a sand prairie, a hummingbird garden, and karst topography with sinkholes and a losing stream. Visitors have the opportunity to fish in the kids-only fishing pond, observe wildlife both inside and outside, and hike one of the trails on the White Oak Trace.

White-tailed deer, coyotes, red fox, gray squirrels, raccoons, woodpeckers, hummingbirds, purple martins and bluebirds are common occurrences on the trails and around the nature center. Amphibians, reptiles, and aquatic invertebrates also are a treat for those who trek to the marsh and pond habitats.

The **White Oak Trace** trail system consists of three 0.5-mile loops: **Tulip Poplar Hill**, **Sinkhole Bottom** and **Paw Paw Valley**. The trails meander through the rolling hills of the predominantly oak-hickory forest by means of bridges and a gravel tread. Tulip poplar, sycamore, sassafras, elm, pawpaw, musclewood, basswood, dogwood, redbud and persimmon abound within the variety of oaks and hickories. Devil's walking stick is an unusual tree species that can be found in multiple locations within the trail system. Tulip Poplar Hill begins to the left of the nature center entrance and allows visitors to traverse steep, wooded hillsides along a streambed where woodpeckers and raccoons enjoy spending time. Sinkhole Bottom provides an up-close and personal view of several sinkholes, the losing stream, and a large patch of pokeweed that is found adjacent to a beautiful, wooded hillside. Paw Paw Valley is a more gently sloping section of the trail that provides visitors with a glimpse of pawpaws and Christmas ferns as they travel over the losing stream and areas where water has left its mark. The **Ridgetop Trail's** surface is asphalt, and this flat 0.25-mile section of the trail leads hikers from the back door of the nature center to Farkleberry Knob. At the top of this knoll, named for the farkleberry trees that grow nearby, is an observation deck that provides a bird's eye view of the forest layers.

For an extended walk, visitors can take a short connection called **Cypress Crossing**, a trail segment that connects the White Oak Trace system to the adjacent **Maple Hollow Trail**. Cypress Crossing runs along a hillside just behind the southeast regional office through native grasses and then by an existing amphibian pool. Maple Hollow Trail is a 1-mile loop with numbered stops and an interpretive trail guide that is available at the nature center.

The Cape Girardeau Conservation Campus includes interactive exhibits highlighting the region's forest, marsh, swamp and big river habitats. The building also houses a 160-seat auditorium, three classrooms, a scientific research laboratory and restrooms. Educational and nature-related items are available for sale. The nature center has regularly scheduled public programs and guided walks. The facility is open Tuesday through Saturday from 8 a.m. to 5 p.m. and Sundays from noon to 5 p.m. Pets are not permitted on this area.

Location: In Cape Girardeau from I-55, take the Kingshighway Road exit (Exit 99) and travel east 0.5 mile to the entrance for North County Park on the left.

Contact: Cape Girardeau Conservation Campus Nature Center, 2289 County Park Drive, Cape Girardeau 63701, 573-290-5218

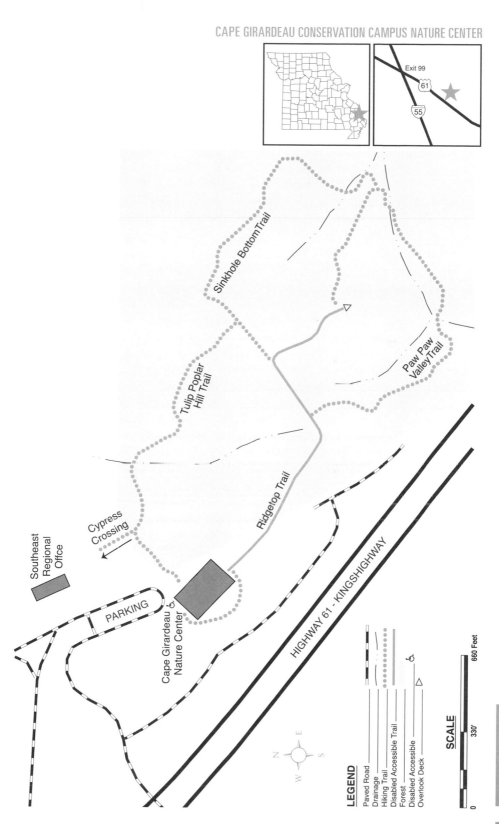

Exit 99

Sinkhole Bottom Trail

Tulip Poplar Hill Trail

Paw Paw Valley Trail

Ridgetop Trail

Cypress Crossing

Southeast Regional Office

PARKING

Cape Girardeau Nature Center

HIGHWAY 61 - KINGSHIGHWAY

LEGEND

Paved Road
Drainage
Hiking Trail
Disabled Accessible Trail
Forest
Disabled Accessible
Overlook Deck

SCALE

0   330'   660 Feet

✳ KETCHERSIDE MOUNTAIN CONSERVATION AREA

Ketcherside Mountain Conservation Area contains 4,877 acres of oak-hickory and mixed-pine forest. Spread out in several sections across Iron and Reynolds Counties, the conservation area is in a beautiful, rugged part of the St. Francois Mountains.

At the eastern edge of one of the most scenic sections of the **Ozark Trail**, this 3.2-mile trail segment on the conservation area is adjacent to Taum Sauk Mountain State Park and the highest point in Missouri. It offers a challenging hike, with steep climbs and loose rock along parts of the route. From the main parking lot along Highway 21, a narrow path heads west into the forest. Winding along contours of the mountain, it turns northward after about 1 mile when it nears Claybaugh Creek. From there the trail climbs another 600 feet as it reaches the end point on Russell Mountain. Watch for warblers in the summer and Cooper's hawk and hermit thrush in the winter.

Hikers starting from the Russell Mountain trailhead at the north end of the trail need travel only a short distance before reaching numerous glades waiting to be explored. Watch for lizards on the glades and enjoy panoramic views of the surrounding mountains before descending into the forest. A bit further south is the junction where the Ozark Trail heads west across Taum Sauk Mountain on its way to Johnson's Shut-ins State Park. This is a primitive trail so keep an eye out for the white and green Ozark Trail markers on trees along the route.

Horseback riding and bicycling are not allowed on this section of the Ozark Trail. Primitive camping is permitted. There is a campground, picnic area and restrooms at Taum Sauk Mountain State Park at the end of Route CC. Don't miss a stop at Royal Gorge Natural Area just south of the Claybaugh Creek parking lot on the opposite side of the highway. This unique area is managed to preserve its natural geological and associated plant communities. Big Creek flows rapidly through the Royal Gorge to carve unusual patterns in the granite.

Location: From Ironton, take Highway 21 south 5 miles to the Claybaugh Creek parking lot on the west side of the highway. To reach an alternate parking area at the upper end of this linear trail (Russell Mountain trailhead), take Route CC west approximately 1.5 miles and look for a small pull-off on the left side of the road.

Contact: Southeast Regional Office, 573-290-5730

To
Ironton

21

CC

LEGEND

Boundary
Paved Road
Gravel Road
Parking Lot
Forest
Hiking Trail

N
E
S
W

SCALE

0   1/4   1/2   1 MILE

CC
21
AREA
AA
Hogan
49
21
Glover
E

✳ MILLSTREAM GARDENS CONSERVATION AREA

The St. Francis River flows through this 612-acre scenic tract of land in Madison County. The river and its wooded corridor are part of Missouri's natural area system. The spectacular Tiemann Shut-ins—igneous rocks carved by the river—are within the area's boundaries. Woodlands here are composed of oak, hickory and pine in the uplands, with ash, elm and maple along the river border and its drainages.

The disabled-accessible **Tiemann Shut-ins Hiking Trail**, with its many switchbacks and benches, winds about 1 mile through forest cover. The asphalt trail ends at the Cat's Paw viewing platform that overlooks the shut-ins on the St. Francis River. Allow 30 minutes one way for the paved section of trail. From the viewing platform, you may follow a natural-surface trail upriver through forest and along pine-covered bluffs above the river. The path ends at a second parking lot and picnic shelter.

For a longer hike, head downriver from the end of the paved trail and follow a **natural-surface trail** along an old roadbed. You will travel parallel to the river and pass two more scenic overlooks. The path then narrows and turns into the forest. After about 0.5 mile the trail leaves the conservation area and enters Forest Service land. Soon you will notice an old foundation and unmarked path on the right. Take this short detour to view a quiet pool at a wide section of the river. The linear trail continues another 0.5 mile to a picnic area at the Silver Mines Recreation Area. From there, the trail extends farther south along the river.

There is a disabled-accessible privy at the trailhead parking lot, and a disabled-accessible privy and picnic shelter at the second parking area. This stretch of river at Millstream Gardens is the only whitewater in Missouri, and kayakers gather here to run the river each spring. Paddlers attempting to float the shut-ins should be prepared with adequate experience and whitewater equipment. Life vests are a necessity, and wetsuits should be worn to prevent hypothermia.

Location: From Fredericktown, follow Highway 72 west for 8.5 miles to the area welcome sign, turn left on the gravel road, then left again at the sign indicating the first parking lot.

Contact: Southeast Regional Office, 573-290-5730

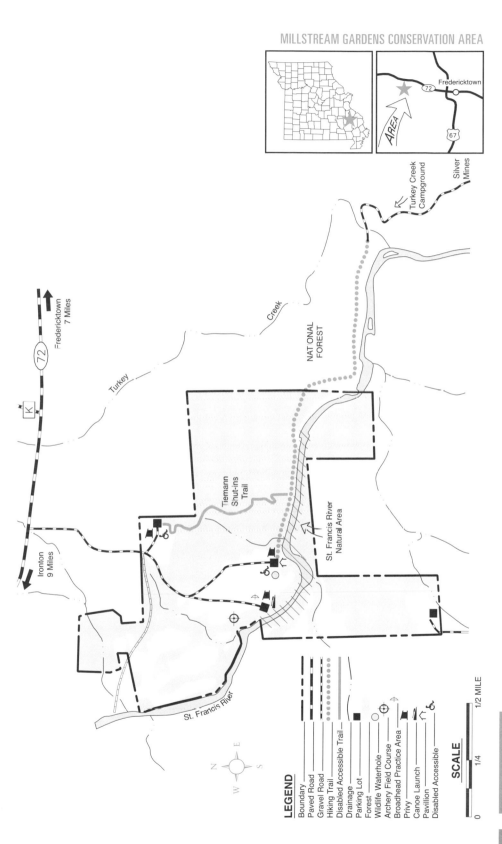

MILLSTREAM GARDENS CONSERVATION AREA

Fredericktown

Turkey Creek Campground

Silver Mines

Fredericktown 7 Miles

72

K

Ironton 9 Miles

Turkey

Creek

NATIONAL FOREST

Tiemann Shut-ins Trail

St. Francis River Natural Area

St. Francis River

N
E
S
W

LEGEND

Boundary
Paved Road
Gravel Road
Hiking Trail
Disabled Accessible Trail
Drainage
Forest
Parking Lot
Wildlife Waterhole
Archery Field Course
Broadhead Practice Area
Privy
Canoe Launch
Pavillion
Disabled Accessible

SCALE

0   1/4   1/2 MILE

PERRY COUNTY COMMUNITY LAKE

Just west of Perryville lies this 103-acre lake, which was created by damming a branch of Saline Creek. The lake is surrounded by old fields and forest land. Additional trees were planted to protect the watershed, provide limited wildlife browse and cover, and for aesthetic reasons. You may see deer, turkey, squirrels, quail, rabbits, beavers, shorebirds, ducks, geese and a variety of songbirds on this 310-acre area. During the winter months, you may spot an eagle. The lake offers good angling opportunities for largemouth bass, bluegill, channel catfish and redear sunfish.

The **Shoreline Trail** is a 4-mile loop around the lake. Most of this wide grass and dirt trail is through forest. Benches along the route provide plenty of opportunities to stop and enjoy lake views from various vantage points. From the parking lot, head across the earthen dam and into the woods where the path weaves along the west side of the lake. At the lake's south end it is necessary to walk along a county road and then north along the conservation area access road, until you reach a parking lot on the southeast side of the area. On the far end of the parking lot, the trail picks up again and leads back into the woods. The path follows the east side of the lake, emerging at the north end near the disabled-accessible fishing pier. Follow the gravel road back to the main parking area. Allow one and a half to two hours for this easy hike. Due to the proximity of the interstate highway, expect to hear some of its noise during your hike.

Picnic areas may be found near the main parking lot and a second parking lot on the southeast side of the lake. There is a privy and a boat ramp at each of these parking areas. An additional parking area and a disabled-accessible fishing pier are adjacent to the main lot. Off the southern tip of the area is a small parking lot with an archery target range across the road. Camping is not permitted at the lake, but a nearby KOA campground trail connects to the Shoreline Trail.

Location: At the junction of I-55 and Highway 51 in Perryville, take Highway 51 north 1 mile, then travel west on Route T for 1.6 miles. At the conservation area sign, turn left on County Road 700, then left again to the parking area.

Contact: Southeast Regional Office, 573-290-5730

55 Perryville
51
61
AREA
T
E
K
B
51

T

Perryville - 1 Mile →

55

Perry Co. Road 700

Hunt. Br.

Perry
County
Community
Lake

Perry Co. Road 702

Archery
Range

LEGEND

Boundary	
Paved Road	
Gravel Road	
Hiking Trail	
Drainage	
Parking Lot	
Privy	
Boat Ramp	
Picnic Area	
Fishing Pier	
Fishing Jetty	
Forest	
Disabled Accessible	&.

N
W — E
S

SCALE

0   1/8   1/4 MILE

SOUTHEAST

91

☀ PICKLE SPRINGS NATURAL AREA

The waters of Pickle Springs flow through this enchanting 256-acre natural area and national natural landmark. The site offers spectacular views from tall sandstone bluffs. It is home to several rare plants and interesting geologic features. The rocks here were formed nearly 500 million years ago when sand deposited in an extensive maze of braided river channels was cemented together to form sandstone. Throughout time, parts of the sandstone has been worn away by water, ice, rain, wind and plants, creating fantastic formations and deep, cool, moist canyons.

Natural features on the area include moist and dry sandstone cliffs and a sandstone glade. Pickle Springs also contains a headwaters stream, sandstone savanna, sandstone talus and sandstone forest. Look for wild azaleas in the spring, and rattlesnake plantain, partridge berry, farkleberry and lowbush blueberry in the summer. The area's waterfalls are dazzling after a rain. Moist soils along the creeks nurture cinnamon, maidenhair and hay-scented fern, and sphagnum moss. Watch for fence lizards, five-lined skinks, box turtles and leopard frogs among the rocks in summer.

The **Trail Through Time** is a 2-mile natural-surface loop. Self-guided trail brochures are available at the trailhead, and most features are identified by wood signs. Hikers will pass waterfalls, rock shelters, a double arch, towering bluffs, canyons and amazing rock outcrops. The trail approaches steep cliffs and bluffs, so use caution and stay on the designated path at all times. Follow the trail clockwise, passing through and around features such as the Slot, Cauliflower Rocks and the Keyhole. Bridges make for easy crossings of Pickle and Bone creeks.

Spirit Canyon is about two-thirds of the way around the loop. The sun never reaches the bluff shelter here, where moisture and acid conditions allow mosses and liverworts to thrive on the shelter walls. At Headwall Falls near the end of the trail, a short spur leads to a viewing platform overlooking a small box canyon.

Bring your camera, and allow two hours to explore this area. There are no facilities at the parking lot. Camping, rock climbing, bicycling and horseback riding are not permitted. Please do not disturb animals, plants or rock formations.

Location: From the junction of Highway 32 and Route W in Farmington, travel east on Highway 32 for 5 miles, then east on Route AA for 1.7 miles to Dorlac Road. Turn left and drive 0.4 mile to the parking lot on the right.

Contact: Southeast Regional Office, 573-290-5730

NATURAL AREA

Trail
Through
Time

AA

Dorlac Road

SCALE

0   1/8   1/4   1/2 MILE

N
E
S
W

LEGEND

Boundary
Paved Road
Gravel Road
Hiking Trail
Drainage
Parking Lot
Forest

SOUTHEAST

93

TYWAPPITY COMMUNITY LAKE

This 184-acre conservation area was acquired in 1957 and features a 37-acre manmade lake. Area management is directed toward protecting the watershed and providing recreational opportunities. A wide variety of tree, shrub and plant life helps support a diversity of wildlife. Species include white oak, northern red oak, black oak, yellow poplar, sweet gum, American beech, cucumber tree, sugar maple, hickory, hop hornbeam, dogwood, redbud and giant cane. Wildflowers include spring beauty and wild ginger.

The 2.5-mile **Tywappity Trail** makes a loop around the entire lake. Almost all of this natural-surface hiking trail is through forest. The trail begins at the north end of the parking lot and weaves around arms of the lake—first along the west and then the east side. Bridges along the way make it easy to cross the low areas and drainages without getting your feet wet.

On the far side of the lake, and visible across the lake from the parking lot, is a corner of land with two benches. A spur trail leads from the main loop down to this point—a nice spot to rest and take in the scenery before continuing your hike. At the southeast edge of the lake, the trail comes out of the woods. Walk across the earthen dam back to the parking area. A few steep sections along the trail make this a moderate hike of about one and a half hours.

Camping is not permitted on this area. Disabled-accessible privies and a pavilion are off the parking lot. Grills and picnic tables are available, as is a boat ramp and disabled-accessible fishing dock.

Location: From Cape Girardeau, take I-55 south to Route M (Exit 89), then go 7 miles west to Route A. Turn left, then left again on Route RA. Follow RA north 1 mile to the parking area.

Contact: Southeast Regional Office, 573-290-5730

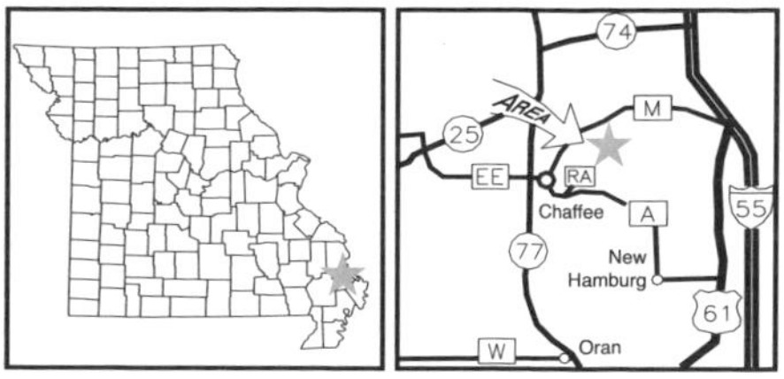

74

Area

25 **M**

EE **RA**

Chaffee **A**

77 **55**

New
Hamburg

61

W Oran

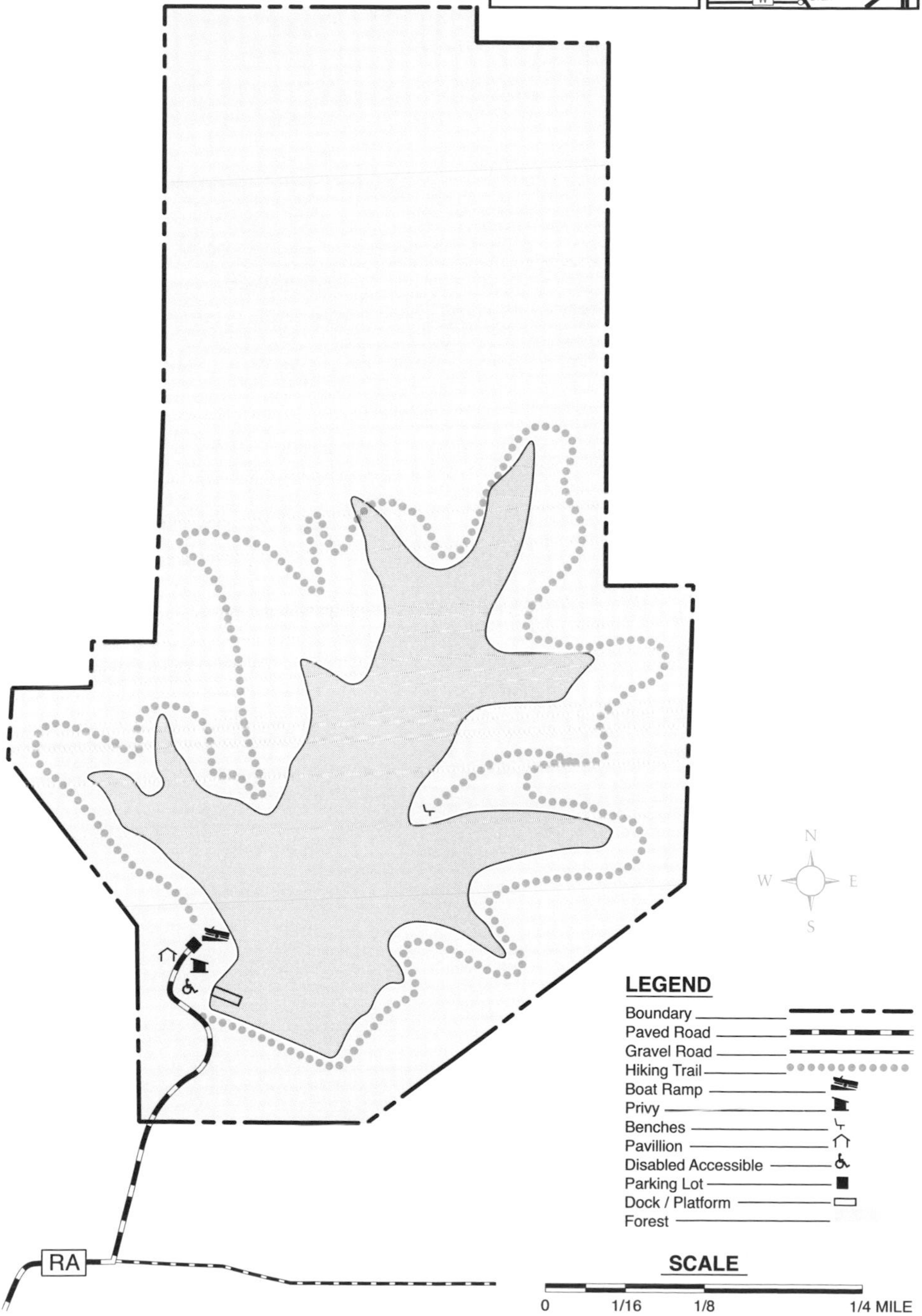

N

W E

S

LEGEND

Boundary
Paved Road
Gravel Road
Hiking Trail
Boat Ramp
Privy
Benches
Pavillion
Disabled Accessible
Parking Lot
Dock / Platform
Forest

SCALE

0   1/16   1/8   1/4 MILE

RA

SOUTHEAST

LIST OF ALL TRAILS ON CONSERVATION DEPARTMENT AREAS

Below is a list of all conservation areas that have maintained trails. Areas featured in this book are listed below in bold type. Trail length is given in miles. For directions and more details on the following areas, call the regional office for an area brochure or visit www.missouriconservation.org.

AC .... Access
CA .... Conservation Area
CL........................... Community Lake
CNC........Conservation Nature Center

CSC .... Conservation Service Center
NA.................................... Natural Area
SF...State Forest
WA .... Wildlife Area

Area Name	County	Trail Type	Length
NORTHWEST REGION			
Bluffwoods CA	**Buchanan**	**disabled-accessible**	**0.5**
Bluffwoods CA	**Buchanan**	**hike**	**0.8**
Bluffwoods CA	**Buchanan**	**hike**	**4.5**
Bonanza CA	Caldwell	hike/bike/horse	3.5
Brickyard Hill CA	Atchison	hike	1.0
Brown (Bob) CA	Holt	disabled-accessible	0.2
Bunch Hollow CA	Carroll	hike/bike/horse	4.5
Fountain Grove CA	Linn/Livingston	disabled-accessible	0.4
Fountain Grove CA	Linn/Livingston	hike	0.6
Fountain Grove CA	Linn/Livingston	hike	2.4
Honey Creek CA	Andrew	hike/bike/horse	13.0
Nodaway County CL	**Nodaway**	**hike**	**2.5**
Pony Express Lake CA	DeKalb	hike	0.5
Pony Express Lake CA	DeKalb	hike	1.0
Poosey CA	**Livingston**	**hike/bike**	**5.0**
Poosey CA	**Livingston**	**hike/bike/horse**	**20.0**
Riverbreaks CA	Holt	hike	4.0
Riverbreaks CA	Holt	hike/bike/horse	4.0
Yellow Creek CA	Chariton	hike	0.5
Yellow Creek CA	Chariton	hike	1.6
Youngdahl (Mark) Urban CA	Buchanan	disabled-accessible	1.4
Youngdahl (Mark) Urban CA	Buchanan	hike	0.7
NORTHEAST REGION			
Big Creek CA	Adair	hike/bike	0.7
Deer Ridge CA	Lewis	hike/bike/horse	19.0
Elmslie Memorial CA	Marion	hike	0.7

Area Name	County	Trail Type	Length
Heath (Charlie) Memorial CA	Clark	hike/bike/horse	5.0
Sever (Henry) Lake CA	Knox	hike/horse	8.5
Steyermark (Julian) Woods CA	Marion	hike	1.0
Sugar Creek CA	**Adair**	**hike**	**2.0**
Sugar Creek CA	**Adair**	**hike/bike/horse**	**10.0**
KANSAS CITY REGION			
Big Buffalo Creek CA	Benton	hike	5.0
Bridger (Jim) Urban CA	Jackson	hike	0.5
Burr Oak Woods CA	**Jackson**	**disabled-accessible**	**0.7**
Burr Oak Woods CA	**Jackson**	**hike**	**0.5**
Burr Oak Woods CA	**Jackson**	**hike**	**1.3**
Burr Oak Woods CA	**Jackson**	**hike**	**1.5**
Burr Oak Woods CA	**Jackson**	**hike**	**3.3**
Clinton CSC	Henry	hike	2.0
Gorman (The Anita B.) Conservation Discovery Center	Jackson	disabled-accessible	0.5
Lipton CA	Jackson	hike	0.5
Little Bean Marsh CA	Platte	disabled-accessible	0.7
Maple Woods NA	**Clay**	**hike**	**1.4**
Montrose CA	Henry	hike	0.9
Montrose CA	Henry	hike	1.2
Parma Woods Range	Platte	hike	1.3
Reed (James A.) Memorial WA	**Jackson**	**hike**	**2.5**
Reed (James A.) Memorial WA	**Jackson**	**hike/bike/horse**	**15.0**
Rush Creek CA	Clay	disabled-accessible	0.5
Rush Creek CA	Clay	hike	1.4
Schell-Osage CA	St. Clair/Vernon	hike	2.5
White Alloe Creek CA	Platte	hike	1.0
CENTRAL REGION			
Bennitt (Rudolf) CA	Howard/Randolph	hike/bike/horse	10.0
Camdenton CSC	**Camden**	**disabled-accessible**	**0.1**
Camdenton CSC	**Camden**	**hike**	**1.1**
Clifty Creek CA	Maries	hike	0.3
Danville CA	Montgomery	hike	3.0
Diana Bend CA	**Howard**	**disabled-accessible**	**0.1**
Diana Bend CA	**Howard**	**hike**	**0.1**

Area Name	County	Trail Type	Length
Eagle Bluffs CA	Boone	hike	3.0
Eagle Bluffs CA	Boone	hike	0.3
Fiery Fork CA	Camden	hike	1.0
Gale (Larry R.) AC	Camden	hike	0.9
Grand Bluffs CA	**Montgomery**	**hike**	**1.0**
Hart Creek CA	Boone	hike/bike	2.0
Hinkson Woods CA	Boone	hike/bike	0.5
Lick Creek CA	Boone	hike	1.0
Little Dixie Lake CA	**Callaway**	**disabled-accessible**	**0.4**
Little Dixie Lake CA	**Callaway**	**hike**	**4.5**
Little Dixie Lake CA	**Callaway**	**hike/bike**	**6.0**
Painted Rock CA	**Osage**	**hike**	**1.6**
Prairie Home CA	Cooper/Moniteau	hike	8.0
Prairie Home CA	Cooper/Moniteau	hike/bike/horse	6.0
Runge CNC	**Cole**	**disabled-accessible**	**0.3**
Runge CNC	**Cole**	**hike**	**2.1**
Scrivner Road CA	**Cole**	**hike/horse**	**8.5**
Smith (Roger V. & Viola W.) CA	Cole/Moniteau	hike	0.2
Three Creeks CA	Boone	hike	3.0
Three Creeks CA	Boone	hike/bike/horse	8.0

ST. LOUIS REGION

Area Name	County	Trail Type	Length
Bellefontaine CA	**St. Louis**	**disabled-accessible**	**0.3**
Bellefontaine CA	**St. Louis**	**hike**	**1.7**
Bootleg AC	Washington	hike	1.5
Busch (August A.) Memorial CA	St. Louis	hike	0.2
Busch (August A.) Memorial CA	St. Louis	hike	0.2
Busch (August A.) Memorial CA	St. Louis	hike	0.2
Busch (August A.) Memorial CA	St. Louis	hike	0.4
Busch (August A.) Memorial CA	St. Louis	hike	0.4
Busch (August A.) Memorial CA	St. Louis	hike	0.7
Busch (August A.) Memorial CA	St. Louis	hike/bike	3.2
Columbia Bottom CA	**St. Louis**	**hike**	**3.0**
Columbia Bottom CA	**St. Louis**	**hike/bike**	**4.7**
Daniel Boone CA	Warren	hike/bike/horse	5.0
Emmenegger Nature Park	**St. Louis**	**disabled-accessible**	**0.5**
Emmenegger Nature Park	**St. Louis**	**hike**	**1.0**
Engelmann Woods NA	Franklin	hike	1.5

Area Name	County	Trail Type	Length
Forest 44 CA	St. Louis	disabled-accessible	0.4
Forest 44 CA	St. Louis	hike	2.2
Forest 44 CA	St. Louis	hike/horse	11.6
Hickory Woods CA	St. Louis	hike	1.5
Howell Island CA	St. Charles	hike/bike	8.0
Hughes Mountain NA	Washington	hike	1.4
Huzzah CA	Crawford	hike	7.0
Klamberg (Roger) Woods CA	St. Louis	hike	0.7
Klamberg (Roger) Woods CA	St. Louis	hike/bike	0.7
Little Indian Creek CA	Franklin	hike/horse	12.1
Little Lost Creek CA	Warren	hike	1.3
Little Lost Creek CA	Warren	hike/bike/horse	5.8
Long Ridge CA	Franklin	hike/horse	9.5
Meramec CA	Franklin	disabled-accessible	1.3
Meramec CA	Franklin	hike	0.1
Meramec CA	Franklin	hike	5.5
Meramec CA	Franklin	hike/bike/horse	10.5
Powder Valley CNC	St. Louis	disabled-accessible	0.3
Powder Valley CNC	St. Louis	hike	0.7
Powder Valley CNC	St. Louis	hike	1.2
Reifsnider (Frank) SF	Warren	hike	1.3
Rockwoods Range	St. Louis	hike	1.3
Rockwoods Range	St. Louis	hike	2.5
Rockwoods Range	St. Louis	hike/bike/horse	7.1
Rockwoods Reservation	St. Louis	disabled-accessible	0.1
Rockwoods Reservation	St. Louis	hike	0.1
Rockwoods Reservation	St. Louis	hike	1.5
Rockwoods Reservation	St. Louis	hike	2.0
Rockwoods Reservation	St. Louis	hike	2.0
Rockwoods Reservation	St. Louis	hike	2.2
Rockwoods Reservation	St. Louis	hike	3.2
Saint Stanislaus CA	St. Louis	disabled-accessible	0.4
Saint Stanislaus CA	St. Louis	hike	3.5
Valley View Glades NA	Jefferson	hike	2.5
Victoria Glades CA	Jefferson	hike	2.3
Weldon Spring CA	St. Charles	hike	5.3
Weldon Spring CA	St. Charles	hike	8.2

Area Name	County	Trail Type	Length
Weldon Spring CA	**St. Charles**	**hike/bike**	**8.0**
Weldon Spring CA	**St. Charles**	**hike/bike**	**10.0**
Young CA	Jefferson	hike	2.5
SOUTHWEST REGION			
Bicentennial CA	Newton	disabled-accessible	0.8
Bicentennial CA	Newton	hike/bike/horse	4.5
Bois D'Arc CA	Greene	hike	5.0
Boston Ferry CA	Taney	hike	0.5
Buffalo Hills NA	McDonald	hike	2.0
Bushwhacker Lake CA	Vernon	hike/bike/horse	6.0
Busiek SF & WA	**Christian**	**hike/bike/horse**	**8.0**
Busiek SF & WA	**Christian**	**hike/bike/horse**	**10.0**
Compton Hollow CA	**Webster**	**hike/bike/horse**	**5.5**
Davis (Lester R.) Memorial Forest	Barton	hike/bike	3.0
Flag Spring CA	Barry/McDonald	hike/bike/horse	11.3
Fort Crowder CA	Newton	hike	0.7
Fort Crowder CA	Newton	hike/bike/horse	11.0
Henning (Ruth and Paul) CA	**Taney**	**hike**	**0.4**
Henning (Ruth and Paul) CA	**Taney**	**hike**	**1.8**
Henning (Ruth and Paul) CA	**Taney**	**hike**	**3.4**
Huckleberry Ridge CA	McDonald	hike/bike/horse	17.4
Lead Mine CA	Dallas	hike	0.5
Lead Mine CA	Dallas	hike/bike/horse	22.2
Little Sac Woods CA	Greene	hike	7.0
Pilot Knob CA	**Stone**	**hike**	**2.7**
Pleasant Hope CA	Polk	hike	1.7
Pleasant Hope CA	Polk	hike/bike/horse	7.7
Shepherd of the Hills Fish Hatchery	Taney	hike	0.4
Shepherd of the Hills Fish Hatchery	Taney	hike	0.7
Shepherd of the Hills Fish Hatchery	Taney	hike	1.6
Springfield CNC	**Greene**	**hike**	**2.8**
Stockton Reservoir	Dade	hike	1.1
Stockton Reservoir	Dade	hike/bike/horse	14.0
Talbot (Robert E.) CA	Lawrence	hike	2.1
Talbot (Robert E.) CA	Lawrence	hike/bike/horse	11.2
Wire Road CA	Stone	hike	1.0
Wire Road CA	Stone	hike/bike/horse	3.7

Area Name	County	Trail Type	Length
Woods (Walter) CA	Newton	disabled-accessible	0.3
Woods (Walter) CA	Newton	hike	0.7
OZARK REGION			
Angeline CA	**Shannon**	**hike**	**1.0**
Barn Hollow NA	Howell/Texas	hike	0.5
Beaver Creek CA	Phelps	hike	0.2
Boesl (L.A.) Outdoor Education Area	Texas	hike	0.3
Caney Mountain CA	Ozark	hike	0.5
Caney Mountain CA	Ozark	hike	1.5
Davis (Dean) CA	Howell	hike	1.0
Drury-Mincy CA	Taney	hike	0.3
Drury-Mincy CA	Taney	hike	1.5
Ozark Regional Office	Howell	disabled-accessible	0.1
Ozark Regional Office	Howell	hike	0.3
Patrick Bridge AC	Ozark	hike	0.3
Peck Ranch CA	Carter	hike	0.5
Peck Ranch CA	Carter	hike	11.0
Rocky Creek CA	Shannon	hike	9.0
Tingler Prairie CA	**Howell**	**hike**	**2.0**
Vanderhoef (Archie and Gracie) Memorial SF	Howell	hike	0.5
SOUTHEAST REGION			
Allred Lake NA	Butler	hike	0.2
Amidon Memorial CA	**Madison**	**hike**	**1.0**
Apple Creek CA	Cape Girardeau	hike/bike/horse	5.0
Buford Mountain CA	Iron/Washington	hike	10.5
Cape Girardeau Conservation Campus	**Cape Girardeau**	**disabled-accessible**	**0.3**
Cape Girardeau Conservation Campus	**Cape Girardeau**	**hike**	**1.0**
Cape Woods CA	Cape Girardeau	disabled-accessible	0.8
Castor River CA	Bollinger	hike/bike/horse	19.5
General Watkins CA	Scott	hike	1.0
General Watkins CA	Scott	hike	1.5
Hickory Canyons NA	Ste. Genevieve	hike	0.2
Hickory Canyons NA	Ste. Genevieve	hike	1.0
Holly Ridge CA	Stoddard	hike/bike/horse	8.0

Area Name	County	Trail Type	Length
Ketcherside Mountain CA	Iron	hike	3.2
Ketcherside Mountain CA	Reynolds	hike	3.0
Knob Lick Towersite	St. Francois	disabled-accessible	0.1
Lon Sanders Canyon CA	Wayne	hike	0.3
Lon Sanders Canyon CA	Wayne	hike	0.5
Magnolia Hollow CA	Ste. Genevieve	disabled-accessible	0.3
Magnolia Hollow CA	Ste. Genevieve	hike	1.1
Miller CL	Carter	hike	1.0
Millstream Gardens CA	Madison	disabled-accessible	1.0
Millstream Gardens CA	Madison	hike	1.0
Otter Slough CA	Stoddard	hike	1.2
Perry County CL	Perry	hike	4.0
Pickle Springs NA	Ste. Genevieve	hike	2.0
Southeast Regional Office	Cape Girardeau	hike	0.5
Tower Rock NA	Perry	hike	0.2
Tywappity CL	Scott	hike	2.5
University Forest CA	Butler	hike/bike/horse	19.0